SUNK WITHOUT TRACE

25/5/m
20,—

SUNK
WITHOUT
TRACE

SOME FORGOTTEN
MASTERPIECES RECONSIDERED
THE CLARK LECTURES
1960–1961

ROBERT BIRLEY

London:
Rupert Hart-Davis
1962

c

Printed in Great Britain by Robert MacLehose & Co. Ltd
The University Press, Glasgow

All, all, must perish; but, surviving last,
The love of letters half preserves the past.
True, some decay, yet not a few revive:
Though those shall sink, which now appear to thrive,
As custom arbitrates, whose shifting sway
Our life and language must alike obey.

Byron, *Hints from Horace*

Contents

Preface

I should like first to express my great appreciation of the honour paid me by the Master and Fellows of Trinity College, Cambridge in inviting me — no poet or literary critic, like my predecessors, but a schoolmaster — to give the Clark Lectures. The names of previous lecturers were indeed intimidating, but if anything could have put me at my ease it was the hospitality extended me by the College, for which I am most grateful. No one coming from Eton can ever feel quite a stranger at Trinity. He comes from a place which has produced — and is still producing — so much of the raw material of that great College. If he walks across the Great Court, the odds are that he will see a familiar face. This old and happy association made me appreciate my privilege and the kindness shown me all the more. I am grateful also to the audience for the encouragement they gave me.

These lectures owe most to two great libraries. It was in the College Library at Eton that I found some years ago a copy of the original edition of Robert Allott's *England's Parnassus*, in which I read the extracts from Warner's *Albions England* that first made me want to discover how this poem could once have been so popular. In the London Library was a copy of the poem itself, the final edition of 1612. Is there in the world another library from which one could take out a copy of *Albions England* and read it, as I have suggested it should be read, in bed? In Eton College Library I could find the Chronicles which Warner used, the religious and scientific tracts read by Edward Young, and very nearly every book referred to in the footnotes of Robertson's *Charles V*. Between them the two libraries have most of the works of oriental history and travel which Thomas Moore consulted while he was writing *Lalla Rookh*. That the London Library should have so many of the invaluable critical works on English Literature published in America, to which due acknowledgment is made in my footnotes, experience had led me to expect. Nor was I surprised to find the poems of the now forgotten Spasmodic School so well represented there. But who on earth could have imagined that he would find in it, for instance, Sir Charles Cotterell's enormous folio translation of la Calprenède's novel, *Cassandre*, printed in 1667? I have learnt, however, that it is always worth looking up the Catalogue of the London Library, however little one expects success. The libraries of the British Museum and the great Universities were a completely dependable and very necessary last line of retreat. But a much occupied amateur needed to be able to take the books home, and without the London Library these lectures could never have been prepared.

I should like to thank my friend and colleague, Mr Oliver Van Oss, Lower Master of Eton, for introducing me to the passage from Paul Valéry which I have quoted at the end of the book. It nearly made me write to my hosts and ask leave to change the subject of the lectures. He made amends by producing the translation I have used. Only those who know the original can realise how impossibly difficult it must have been and how beautifully it was done. And, finally, while it is the recognised lot of the wives of writers to read through their husband's books in typescript, the wife of this one has done more. She listened patiently to each lecture being read to her, greatly to the benefit of its official audience.

R.B.

I

William Warner
Albions England

'O vannagloria dell' umane posse' — 'O how meaningless the
great reputations men gain by their abilities!' cried out
the celebrated painter, Oderisi of Gubbio, among the proud on
the Mount of Purgatory, as he pointed out to Dante that men
had now come to think more of his contemporary and rival,
Franco Bolognese, than of himself. 'Cimabue was thought
to lead the field in painting and now all acclaim Giotto. In
just the same way, one Guido has supplanted another as the
glory of our tongue and who knows that there is not someone alive now who will turn them both out of the nest. Fame
on earth is nothing but a breath of wind, coming now hence,
now thence, and it changes its name because it changes its
direction.'

I shall be speaking to you of the changing fame or reputation
of six works of literature, five poems and one history. Perhaps
my title may go too far, for historians of English Literature
occasionally drop a buoy or two round the scene of the wrecks
and sometimes divers go down and have a look at the wrecks
themselves. But I have adopted one test for the six works that I
have chosen and I think all six pass it successfully. They were
once read and admired by men of taste and education; they are
not read now.

Of course, one never quite knows. The revival of an appreciation of Herrick, almost totally unread for over a hundred years
after his death, began when an inquirer wrote to the *Gentleman's
Magazine* in 1796 to ask for information about a poet, of whom

he had never heard before, the author of a book called
Hesperides, which had been published in 1648. Herrick must
now be one of the most remorselessly anthologised of all
English poets. In 1800 Wordsworth noted what was he thought
the final disappearance of a once very famous galleon: 'the
verses of Dryden, once highly celebrated, are forgotten.' But
I doubt whether any of the ships of which I shall be speaking will ever appear, like Herrick or Dryden, on the Register
again.

Porson — or rather, Porson as improved by Byron — once
spoke of poems which 'will be read when Homer and Virgil are
forgotten, but — not till then'. Being forgotten, however, is
not quite the same thing as not being read. A poem may be
remembered, may indeed be very influential, without being
read. It almost seems as though it does not matter so much
if the very greatest authors are not read. They can carry on
their work as the foundations of a whole literary culture for an
astonishingly long time unread. For Dante, Homer was the
sovereign poet; he met him in Limbo, sword in hand, moving
before Horace, Ovid and Lucan as their lord. But Dante had
never read Homer, nor had anyone else in the Italy of his day.
Still, they cannot live quite for ever unread as the acknowledged
lords of writers who *are* read. I rather think that we are now
passing through a period when the greatest classical authors are
changing guard, and that Homer and Virgil have had their day.
They are becoming like the nameless giants, whom all people
believe to have existed in the most distant past, the strong men
who lived before Agamemnon, the shadowy earliest inhabitants of Canaan, whom we meet occasionally in the Old Testa-
ment, the Anakim, the Rephaim or the Zam-Zumim, 'people,
great and tall', or the few giants, whom Geoffrey of Monmouth
tells us Brute, the son of Aeneas, found in this island. Their
places as the great classic writers are being taken by two others
— and they are not unworthy successors — Shakespeare and
Dickens. Perhaps, some centuries hence, the historian of this
cultural revolution will add a footnote to quote as a piece of
minor evidence of its progress the decision of two universities

in England to abandon the study of Latin as a compulsory requirement for admission.

I am not suggesting that any of the six writers of whom I shall speak will be remembered like the Zam-Zumim — except perhaps one, Edward Young. He may survive for some time yet, not altogether forgotten, though unread. But they were all read, and read enthusiastically, in their own day. If we are interested in the past, it may be felt worth while to consider how this could have been.

An author who is no longer read faces a difficulty from which a painter may escape. Gianbattista Tiepolo, regarded at his death as the greatest artist of his time, was completely neglected in the following century. Ruskin, in all his works on Italian painting, spoke of him only once, in a scornful allusion to one of his ceiling-paintings in his guide-book, *St Mark's Rest*. But Tiepolo's great frescoes were still there, waiting to be looked at if they once more became interesting. No publisher had to sink any money in reproducing them. Of the six works with which I shall deal, Lee's *Rival Queens* has recently been reprinted in America in a collected edition of his plays, and two of the stories in *Lalla Rookh* are still obtainable in this country in an edition for schools. None of the rest is in print. Who is likely to risk his capital in publishing them again? A University Press might do so, I suppose, and, indeed, ten years ago we were promised an edition of William Warner's *Albions England* from an American university, though it has not yet appeared. If it does, I do not imagine that it will make much difference. William Warner will not be read.

I had better begin by saying something about him. This will not take long, as very little is known.[1] (I might note at this point that practically everything told us about Warner by Anthony à Wood is demonstrably untrue and may be disregarded.) He was born in 1558. His father had probably accompanied Richard Chancellor on his voyage to Russia in

[1] For William Warner's life see William Warner, *Syrinx*, ed. W. A. Bacon (Evanston, Illinois, 1950), pp. xxx–xli, which supersedes the life in the *D.N.B.*

1553 and certainly died on a voyage to the Gold Coast in 1577. William Warner seems to have been at either Oxford or Cambridge. He writes of

> an Academie, which I reverence so much,
> As gessed against it splenous thoughts me splenously
> would touch,

which must surely have been written by an alumnus. He claims that,

> For as (so Historie) it was the Primer-schooling Heere,
> So ever have Religion and the Muses held it deare.

But a past member of either University would say as much, and in the reign of Elizabeth both Oxford and Cambridge claimed to have been the first to be founded, the 'Primer-schooling'. Our decision between the two must depend on our interpretation of four very confusing lines that follow,

> Not miles from it a Township is, I know not whether in
> A neighbouring Mart more famous, or more infamous for
> sinne
> Of Beggars, Brothels, Cheaters, Bawds, and Vagrants
> once a yeere
> Resorting thither, then to put their sinnes in practice
> there.[1]

What was this Township? Can it be London, as has been suggested? Could a place fifty or sixty miles off be regarded as 'not miles from it'? But, if not London, which would not help us, what can it be? My own guess would be that he is referring in a very muddled way to Stourbridge Fair. If so, Warner was at Cambridge. However, we know that he became an attorney, and that he died at Amwell in Hertfordshire on 9 March, 1609, 'suddenly in his bedde without any former complaynt or sicknesse.' He wrote a romance, called *Syrinx, or a Sevenfold Historie*, published in 1584, which was based on the model of

---

[1] *Albions England. . . . First penned by William Warner: and now revised; and newly enlarged a little before his Death* (London, printed for G. P. and are to be sold by Richard Moore, 1612), Book XV, Chapter 99, pp. 390–1. (All references are to this edition.)

the *Aethiopica* of Heliodorus. He may have been the William
Warner who translated the *Menaechmi* of Plautus in 1595.
And, between 1586 and his death twenty-three years later, he
brought out, in six editions each with revisions and additional
chapters, a long historical poem, which eventually reached to
16 Books or 104 Chapters, more than 12,000 lines in all, called
Albions England. (Albion he explained was the name of the
whole island; England of part of it.) It caused him to be
compared to Homer, Euripides and Virgil.

It is still read sometimes and those who read it seem to derive
no pleasure from the task. Professor Lewis, for instance, gives
us a solemn warning. 'From so vast a poem good phrases can
of course be picked out. . . . But no one should be deceived by
these quotations into reading Warner. The good things in
Albions England are as far divided as the suns in space.'[1]
Dr Tillyard found it equally forbidding: 'In bulk a modern
reader finds this long narrative from Noah to Queen Elizabeth
unreadable; without the grimmest exercise of will he cannot
keep his attention fixed: and pleasure is out of the question.'[2]
As for Dr A. L. Rowse, 'in the end, whatever one's good will,
the lagging fourteener is too much for one.'[3] Professor Lewis
says that Warner 'has been kindly treated both by his contemporaries and by posterity'. George Saintsbury, it is true,
held that 'though he will not bear comparison with the better,
even of the second-rate Elizabethans, the singularity of the
plan of his book, and some vigorous touches here and there,
raise him above the mass'[4] — but that is not noticeably kind.
Only Charles Lamb seems actually to have enjoyed him. 'I
have read Warner with great pleasure. What an elaborate
piece of alliteration and antithesis! Why, it must have been a
labour far above the most difficult versification.'[5]

I cannot help thinking that these modern critics have been

---

[1] C. S. Lewis, *English Literature in the Sixteenth Century* (1954), 465.
[2] E. M. W. Tillyard, *The English Epic and its Background* (1954), 322.
[3] A. L. Rowse, *The England of Elizabeth* (1950), 62.
[4] *The English Poets*, ed. T. H. Ward (1880), I, 431.
[5] *Letters of Charles Lamb*, ed. E. V. Lucas (1935), II, 410.

reading the poem in the wrong way. Perhaps it is the contemporary comparison with Homer that has misled them. Sir Sidney Lee, and more recently Professor Lewis, have pointed out that Warner's model was the *Metamorphoses* of Ovid.[1] It is not an epic; it is a collection of stories in short chapters, bound together, as in Ovid's poem, by a loose thread of continuous narrative, here an historical narrative. It should be read as a bedside book, which is the way in which I have recently been reading it.

Sir Harold Nicolson (I owe this quotation to Mr Wilkinson's delightful book on Ovid[2]) once wrote of the *Metamorphoses*, 'It is as if some bright young man of the twenties had composed a long poem in fifteen books, in which he had interwoven such disparate themes as the Garden of Eden, the Ten Commandments, Samson and Delilah, King Alfred and the Cakes, Drake's drum and the death of Nelson.' This is precisely what William Warner did. He begins with Noah and he ends with Queen Elizabeth. The story of the Tower of Babel is followed at once by that of the birth of Jupiter. We pass quickly to Hercules, whose career occupies nine chapters; a few lines on the fall of Troy and the founding of Rome lead to the early history of our own country, the coming of Brute, the son of Aeneas, to Albion, now named Brutaine, the founding of Troy-novant, later to be called Luds-towne or London, the drowning of 'Sabrin, wondrous faire', the story of 'King Leir and his three daughters'. We come to Julius Caesar, 'the birth of our Saviour Jesus Christ', the conquest of Britain by the Romans, the revolt of Queen Voada and so, by way of King Arthur, the Saxons, the Danes, 'the politicke and couragious Kings Alured and Adelstone', the Norman Conquest, Henry II and Thomas Becket, to the Wars of the Roses and the accession of Henry VII. Something of what happens *en route* may be shown from a recital of the chapter-headings of the sixth book given in a preliminary Table:

[1] Article on William Warner in *D.N.B.*, C. S. Lewis, *op. cit.*, 465.

[2] *The Observer*, 25 June 1950. Review of Rex Warner, *Men and Gods*, quoted in L. P. Wilkinson, *Ovid Recalled* (1955), 151.

Of King Henrie the fourth: of the Rebellions in his time: and of Richard the seconds death.

Of the victorious Prince Henry the fift. Of Queene Katherine and Owen Tudor.

Of the wowing and wedding of Vulcan and Venus: and of the strife betwixt Venus and Phoebus.

How Pan wowed, and was deceived.

Of Mercurie his successlesse love.

Of Mars his censure of love and women: and of Jupiters Sentence and sayings.

Of the troublesome Raigne of King Henry the sixt: how he was lastly deposed: And of King Edward the fourth.

Of King Richard the third, and his Tyrannies.

How Henry Earle of Richmond overcame and slew King Richard the third.

Of the uniting of the two houses Lancaster and Yorke by intermariage.

If you ask how the stories of Vulcan and Venus, of Pan and Mercury, and the sayings of Mars and Jupiter come in, I can only read you the last lines of the twenty-ninth chapter and the first few of the thirtieth. They will give you some idea how he organised his poem. (It should be remembered that for Queen Katherine marriage to Owen Tudor was a *mésalliance*.)

Once, when this Match was at a point, they merrily
    disposed,
Did descant what from vulgar tongues thereof would be
    supposed.
They will beleeve me amorous, or thee so wived as
Vulcan, the Smith of Lemnos, that to Venus married was.
The Queene did say: And Tudor said, I hope of hansell
    better,
In Venus and in Vulcans names more lieth than the letter:
For he was as I would not be, She as you should be never,
Either so apt to give and take as pittie them to sever.
I pray thee, Owen, quoth the Queene, how met they, canst
    thou tell?
I can he said, and more than so, then marke the processe well:

B

When Vulcan was a Batcheler, and Venus was unwed,
Thus wowde he her, thus wonne he her, thus wowde and
    wonne hee sped.
Venus, the fairest Goddesse, and as amorous as faire,
Belov'd of Mars, and loving Mars, made oftentimes repaire
To Vulcans forge, as to see wrought for Jupiter his Fire
And thunders, Mars his Armors, and the Sunwaines curious
    tire,
When they indeed, of merriments in Love did theare
    conspire,
And lastly did conclude the Smith a Stale upon their sport,
Wherein did Venus play her part, prevailing in this sort.[1]

With the accession of Henry VII the second edition of the poem ended. Warner was to continue it until eventually it was nearly two and half times as long. At first it keeps fairly strictly to the historical narrative, though, when telling of Perkin Warbeck, he refers to his love for 'the Earle of Huntlies daughter' and we are then told a story of Erickmon and Ginetta and the tales of 'the Bat and the Moole' and of 'the Cuckowe and the Owle'. However, we then get back into the straight with a chapter entitled, 'Of Empson and Sutton alias Dudley'.

Long before, after dealing with Henry II and Thomas Becket, Warner had written,

The Kings fayre Leiman Rosamund, and how his Sonnes
    rebell
I over-passe. To Richard next the Dyadem befel.[2]

He now makes good this rather surprising omission — in the course of a chapter on Mary Tudor. Although

Queene Mary seem'd to shut up Heaven, and set wide open
    Hell,

he writes of her not unsympathetically: 'her courage', he says, 'was not common.' When she learns that her husband, Philip

---

[1] Book VI, Chapters 29, 30, p. 146.
[2] Book V, Chapter 25, p. 117.

of Spain, was staying in dalliance with 'rich Brabants supreame faire, the Bakers daughter', a friend advises her that Kings are often unfaithful, 'for Kings will shew they raigne'. Thus Edward IV was 'guilty of a Leash of Loves, Shores wife and other twaine', and yet 'lov'd his Queene no whit the lesse', just as, he continues, 'did our second Henry, whom his Queene oft crost in vaine.'[1] The story of Fair Rosamund which follows is well told, especially the climax, though the last line shows Warner at his clumsiest.

> Fair Rosamund surprised thus, eare thus she did suspect,
> Fell on her humble knees, and did her fearefull hands erect.
> She blush't out beauty, whilst the teares did wash her
> pleasing face,
> And begged Pardon, meriting no lesse of common grace.
> So far forth as it in me lay I did, quoth she, withstand,
> But what may not so great a King by meanes or force
> command?
> And durst thou, Minion, quoth the Queene, thus article
> to me,
> That then wert Non-plus when the King commanded Lust to
> thee.
> Nay, best he take thee to the Court, Be thou his Queene,
> do call
> Me to attendance, if his Lust may stand for Law in all.
> I know it Strumpet, so harps he, and thou does hope the
> same:
> But so I live, and live I will, at least to marre that game.
> With that she dasht her on the Lippes, so dyed double red:
> Hard was the heart that gave the blow, soft were those lips
> that bled.
> Then forced she to swallow downe (prepar'd for that intent)
> A poisoned Potion: which dispatcht, to whence they came
> they went.[2]

But the poem by this time was getting out of hand. There follows a 'catalogue or Epitome' of English History and 'an

[1] Book VIII, Chapter 41, pp. 197–8.
[2] *Ibid.*, p. 200.

Observation touching this letter H', which from Hercules, through Helen, the British wife of Constantine, Hengest and Horsa, Harold, Hardiknought the Dane and others, down to the eight Henries, proved itself 'ominous to Englands good or ill'. Elizabeth ascends the throne, but we quickly turn to a consideration of 'the untimely ends of most of our English Dukes since the Conquest', and then, as something of a climax, the story of the Armada. This, to tell the truth, is a disappointment, though it is interesting to note that for Warner the most satisfactory feature of that great crisis was the way that the Catholic families of England rallied to her defence. Warner himself was a sturdy Protestant, as some chapters on Spain and the Jesuits now make clear. I believe that a study of Warner's position in the religious controversies of the day would be rewarding. He was a good example of a class who must have been numerous, but who never receive the limelight, like the extremists on either side. He was a solid, middle-of-the-way, Book of Common Prayer man (he had a great admiration for the Prayer Book), equally critical of Papists and Precisians.

There in 1592 the poem ended once more, but four years later he took it up again. He now goes back to the story of Mary Queen of Scots. His attitude towards her may be seen from one of the chapter-headings, 'Of her lawfull and orderly Triall. Of the most deliberate and merciful handling of her cause &c.' Still, while he emphasises her refusal to the last to accept the ministrations of the English clergy, his account of her death is not ungenerous.

That, even then, the Gospels Light illuminate her heart
Was prayd of Ours, whilst she with hers prayd, as pleasde
    her, a-part.
Then to her wofull servants did she passe a kinde a-dew:
And kissing of her Crucifix, unto the block her drew,
And feareles, as if glad to dye, did dye to Papisme trew.
Which, and her other Errors (who in much did ever err)
Unto the Judge of Mercie and of Justice we referre.[1]

[1] Book X, Chapter 56, p. 249.

Then, after a look at the struggles in France and the Low
Countries, interrupted by 'the tragicall historie of King Davids
Children', he strikes a new vein, turning to Hakluyt.[1] Here for
two books he abandons the Ovidian method of narration and
simply swings backwards and forwards between, on the one
hand, the story of Sir John Mandeville, which he places firmly
in the reign of Edward III, and, on the other, the journeys of
five of Hakluyt's voyagers. Of these the first were Sir Hugh
Willoughby and Richard Chancellor, who had set out together
in 1553 to find the North-East Passage. Willoughby and his
companions were frozen to death off the coast of Lapland;
Chancellor returned and three years later tried again and
reached Moscow. There is a chapter on the abortive attempt by
Stephen Burough in the same year, 1556, and then Warner
describes the great journey of Anthony Jenkinson from the
White Sea overland to Persia. This is followed, and it seems
quite incongruously, by the voyage of Robert Macham to
Maderia in the fourteenth century, with references to more
recent English voyages to the East Coast of Africa. Warner's
choice of voyages seems entirely haphazard until we recollect
that his father had been with Chancellor and had died on
Towerson's voyage to the Gold Coast. There is filial as well as
national pride in these books. But the accounts are not much
more than serviceable abridgements of Hakluyt, whom he
follows closely. This is evidence of a slackening of inspiration,
for in the earlier books of the poem Warner did not follow his
authorities at all closely. The story of Fair Rosamund, for
instance, if one compares it with the accounts in the Chronicles,
is found to be quite newly pictured. The tale of Sir John
Mandeville, however, is turned into a romance of his own
invention and a very pleasant one, though it is too long to be
considered here.

In the last book of this edition he gives us his philosophy, or
as he calls it, his 'Physicks and Ethicks against Atheistes and
Epicures, or Natures and Reasons Theologie'. His verse was

[1] R. R. Cawley, 'Warner and the Voyagers' (*Modern Philology*,
1932, XX, 113–47).

quite incapable of carrying more than narrative and description, as these few lines will suffice to show.

> Because of him all Beings be, and he of whom are All
> Ought to be ever, him therefore, Eternall men do call:
> Because to be and not to Live were nothing, and the same
> Whence is all Life should be selfe Life, Him, Living God,
>   they name.
> Because, should Understanding lacke to life, such life were
>   dead,
> And Understanding voyd of Power were lame, and he that
>   bread
> Them both ought in himselfe have both of all, him Men
>   therefore
> Call Might, & Mind: as who would say, al Power &
>   wisedomes stoore.[1]

However, we cannot ignore these tedious chapters. As we shall see, they meant a great deal more to his contemporaries than they ever can to us.

But Warner had not yet finished. In 1606 the poem appeared again, with three more books. There was not much more for him to write about. He was an Elizabethan and the memory of the great Queen still haunted him. It was twenty years since he had published his first four books; in those years English poetry had passed through an unparalleled revolution. In 1586, though Spenser's *Shepherds Calendar* had just appeared, all other English poets were wrestling with the attempt to make their language speak rhythmically at all. Those twenty years had seen the *Faerie Queen*, Marlowe's plays and the poems, the sonnets and early plays of Shakespeare. Just as Warner was bringing his poem to an end Shakespeare was writing *Macbeth*, but Warner, condemned to a metre now abandoned by English poets, was writing,

> I pree thee, Fleance, tell quoth she, which I have heard in
>   part,
> The Storie of the Fairies that foretold thy Fathers fate,

[1] Book XIII, Chapter 79, p. 326.

For why? I know not why, but sure it throbs my heart of late.
Throb may it so it thrive, quoth he, in you to that event
Divind by them, nor hope I you can Destinie prevent:
But howsoever thus it was. King Duncane when alive,
To Makbeth and my father did great Dignities derive;
As chiefest for their births, their wit, and valour, also thay
Held friendship long, and luckely in Scotch affaires did sway.[1]

Warner, it will be seen, was telling the history of Scotland,
appropriate now that a Scotsman was King of England, and for
good measure we are given the history of Wales as well. It
must all have seemed very old-fashioned. However, he apparently still had his readers, as a final edition was published in
1612, after his death.

Warner, who, as I have said, was once compared with Homer
and Euripides, must be considered as a poet, but before I
attempt to do this it may be as well to say something of the
metre he chose for his poem, the 'fourteener'. It is one that it is
very difficult, almost impossible, for us to appreciate.

Let me first take two or three examples from poets other than
Warner to see what could be made of it. First, Richard
Edwards from *The Paradise of Dainty Devices*.

In going to my naked bed, as one that would have slept,
I heard a wife sing to her child, that long before had wept:
She sighed sore and sang full sore, to bring the babe to rest,
That would not rest but cried still in sucking at her breast:
She was full weary of her watch, and grieved with her child,
She rocked it and rated it, until on her it smiled:
Then did she say now have I found the proverb true to prove,
The falling out of faithful friends is the renewing of love.

The fourteener, then, can be quite pointed, though I cannot
help suspecting that there was a certain amount of luck about
that very successful last line, the refrain of the poem. Next,
Robert Southwell.

As I in hoary winter's night stood shivering in snow,
Surprised I was with sudden heat which made my heart to glow;

[1] Book XV, Chapter 94, pp. 376–7.

And lifting up a fearful eye to view what fire was near,
A pretty babe all burning bright did in the air appear,
Who scorched with exceeding heat such floods of tears did
    shed,
As though His floods should quench His flames with what
    His tears were fed.

The fourteener, then, can be used to express a more intense emotion. Or let us take these lines from Chapman's translation of the *Iliad*.

        The winds transferr'd into the friendly sky
Their supper's savour; to the which they sat delightfully,
And spent all night in open field; fires round about them
    shined.
As when about the silver moon, when air is free from wind,
And stars shine clear, to whose sweet beams, high prospects,
    and the brows
Of all steep hills and pinnacles, thrust up themselves for
    shows,
And even the lowly valleys joy to glitter in their sight,
When the unmeasured firmament bursts to disclose her light,
And all the signs in heaven are seen, that glad the shepherd's
    heart;
So many fires disclosed their beams, made by the Trojan
    part,
Before the face of Ilion, and her bright turrets show'd.

Certainly the fourteener can be used for a romantic description. Or this,

While shepherds watch'd their flocks by night, all seated on
    the ground,
The angel of the Lord came down, and glory shone around.

And here, I think, we may see the difficulty. For these, of course, are not fourteeners, but four lines written in Ballad Metre, eight and six, the Common measure of hymns, as familiar to us as any other metrical form. We find the same difficulty with that most ungainly of all Elizabethan metres, the poulter's measure, an Alexandrine followed by a fourteener, which I find

it almost impossible to read aloud. But what of this, the Short
Measure of the Hymn Book?

> Soldiers of Christ arise, and put your armour on,
> Strong in the strength which God supplies and his Eternal
>   Son.

Hymns, of course, are inevitably confusing; we think of them
with their tunes. It needs a considerable detachment to remember, when singing 'Abide with me' at a Cup Final, that it is
written in heroic couplets.

And yet, consider these lines from Warner's poem, when he
writes, in the course of his narrative, of the birth of Christ:

> Augustus, quayling Anthonie, was Emperour alone:
> In whose un-foed Monarchie our common health was knowne.
> The bruser of the Serpents head, the womans promised Seede,
> The Second in the Trinitie, the Foode our soules to feede:
> The Vine, the Light, the Doore, the Way, the Shepheard
>   of us all:
> Whose manhood joynd to Deitie did Ransome us from thrall,
> That was, and is, and evermore will be the same to his,
> That sleepes to none that wake to him, that turns our cursse
>   to blisse,
> Whom yet unseene, the Patriarkes sawe, the Prophets have
>   foretold,
> Th' apostles preacht, the Saints adore, and Martyrs doe
>   behold,
> The same (Augustus Emperour) in Palestine was borne,
> Amongst his owne, and yet his owne did crosse his blisse in
>   scorne.[1]

Do we not find in them something not only of the feeling, but
of the rhythm, of a carol?

But Common Measure, familiar to us not only in hymns, but
in ballads, poems in ballad form, *John Gilpin* or *The Ancient
Mariner*, and in comic poems, is not the fourteener cut into
shorter lines. It is far easier to control. For the rhythm of verse
depends on the management of the lines. Sentences running

[1] Book III, Chapter 18, p. 81.

over the line, by the use of which the speed of a poem can be accelerated or retarded, are comparatively easy to achieve.

> Away went Gilpin, and away
> Went Gilpin's hat and wig;
> He lost them sooner than at first,
> For why? they were too big.

> Now mistress Gilpin, when she saw
> Her husband posting down
> Into the country far away,
> She pull'd out half a crown;

> And thus unto the youth she said
> That drove them to the Bell,
> This shall be yours when you bring back
> My husband safe and well.

In fourteeners running on the sentence is very difficult; enjambment, running it on after the end of the couplet, is almost impossible. Either the line is brought up at a check when you expect it to go on, or the sentence comes to an end too soon in the following line, which then never gets under way at all.

> When arkèd Noah, and seaven with him, the emptyd worlds
>   remain,
> And left the instrumentall meane, of landing them againe,
> And that both man and beast, and all, did multiplie the store,
> To Asia Sem, to Affrick Cham, to Europe Japheth bore
> Their families. Thus triple wise the world devided was.[1]

However, Warner sometimes showed himself capable of giving variety to his rhythm quite effectively by such following on of the sentence.

There is more in Warner's poem than a few good phrases, which is all that Professor Lewis will allow him. These lines, describing the dwelling of Pluto, are a fine piece of descriptive writing, and we may note how, by cutting up the fourth line and introducing an internal rhyme, he overcomes the difficulty I have noted when the sentence is made to run over into the following line:

[1] Book I, Chapter 1, p. 1.

About the desert parts of Greece there is a valley lowe,
To which the roaring waters fall that from the Mountaines
    flowe:
So Rockes doe overshadow it that scarce a man may vewe
The open ayre: no Sun shines there: Amidst this darksome
    Mewe
Doth stand a Citie, to the same belongs one onely Gate,
But one at once may come thereto the entrance is so straite,
Cut out the rough maine stonie Rocke.[1]

What could be livelier than these lines in the story of Narcissus
and Echo?

Meane while the Lad (such power hath pride mens Senses to
    subdue)
Doats on his shadow, now suppos'd to be a Substance true:
And lastly wowes so formally in words and gestures sweete,
That Eccho found his error: and, he saying, Let us meete,
Let's meete, quoth Eccho, mockingly: which, hearing, he
    with speed
(Beleeving that his shadow was a Nymph, and spake in deed,)
Did leape into the Fountaine.[2]

Warner here had Ovid's treatment of the echoing words to
help him, and indeed he refers us to 'Nasoes tale', but a glance
at Golding's famous translation, also in fourteeners, may show
us how neatly in comparison Warner has dealt with his problem.

He still persists, and wondring much what kinde of thing it
    was
From which that answering voyce by turne so duely seemde to
    passe,
Said: let us joyne. She (by hir will desirous to have said,
In fayth with none more willingly at any time or stead)
Said: let us joyne.[3]

---

[1] Book I, Chapter 6, p. 21.   [2] Book IX, Chapter 46, p. 215.
[3] *The XV Bookes of P. Ovidius Naso, entyuled Metamorphosis,
translated by Arthur Golding* (1567), III, 479–83. *Shakespeare's Ovid
being Arthur Golding's Translation of the Metamorphoses,* ed. W. H. D.
Rouse (1904), 72.

Finally, here is what seems to me as successful a piece of
guide-book poetry as one could ask for.

Meane while in Rome (the Misstris once of all the world)
    they view
Such wonders, couch't in ruins, as unseene might seeme
    untrew.
Once it was compast, as is read, with fiftie miles of wall,
Now some to twentie, some to lesse, in that accompt doe fall:
It having Towers so many as the yeare hath dayes in all.
From fortie miles was water brought in Pipes on Arches
    thether.
Were vaulted walkes through every Streete, gainst Sunne,
    & rainy weather.
The sumptious bathes, with Pallaces thereto of rare delight,
The romesom Ponds, where very ships some festivals did fight,
The Trophie Arches, where to life Triumphants were
    purtrade,
The Statures huge, of Porphyrie and costlier matters made,
The Theaters, Pyramides, the Hill of halfe a mile,
Raisde but of tribute Pot-sheards, so to boast their Power
    long while,
The Obelisks, of one whole Stone neere forty yards or more,
Huge Pillers, carv'd in Masonrie with Prowse of Knights
    before,
The stately bridges, sometimes Eight, now fewer, Tyber
    crosse,
The Thirty goodly Gates, of which is now of number losse,
The huge Colosses, Conduites, & else-what shew'd a State
Beyond beleefe of ruin'd Rome, in part repair'd of late,
They wonder at, & how the world could yeeld such Pomp
    debate.
Though some the seaven inclosed Hils did ancient Rome
    containe
Lye waste or Vine-yards, more doth yeat of Maiestie
    remaine,
Even in the Rubble of the old, than in the now renew'd,
Though Rome retaines a Statelines, nor fairer Pyles are
    view'd.

The round Pantheon, once the house of al the Heathen Gods,
Stands yet a Temple, but lesse deckt for rich by too much
    ods.
On Aventine the down-fals are of Temples store to see:
On Tarpie of the Capitol, where wont their Guild to bee:
On Palentine of Pallaces, on Caelius signes of Playes:
Quirinall, Exquell, Viminall, of bathes shew brave decayes.
These Hils, with Vatican and old Janiculum orepast,
Shew we how Rome did rule, was rul'd, and ruin'd at the
    last.[1]

We must consider what Warner meant to his own age. He
was mentioned in some pleasant lines by Henry Chettle from a
poem lamenting the death of Queen Elizabeth.

He that sung fortie yeares her life and birth,
And is by English Albion so much famde
For sweet mixt layes of majestie with mirth,
    Doth of her losse take now but little keepe,
    Or else I gesse he cannot sing, but weepe.[2]

Nash and Drayton complimented him, rather half-heartedly it
must be confessed; the former saying that Poetry 'hath not
beene any whit disparaged by William Warners absolute
Albions',[3] the latter referring to him as 'my old friend'.[4]
Gabriel Harvey spoke of him in company with Sidney, Spenser
and Chapman.[5] But it was in the *Palladis Tamia* of Francis
Meres, written in 1598, that Warner was most highly praised.

At the beginning of the part of his book dealing with modern
English poets, Meres gives lists of the most famous Greek and
Latin poets and then one of those by whom 'the English tongue
is mightily enriched and gorgeously invested in rare ornaments

[1] Book XII, Chapter 73, pp. 300–1.
[2] Henry Chettle, *Englands Mourning Garment*, 1603.
[3] Thomas Nash, 'Preface to Robert Greene's *Menaphon*, 1589'
(*Elizabethan Critical Essays*, ed. G. Gregory Smith (Oxford, 1904), I,
320).
[4] Michael Drayton, *To my most dearely-loved friend Henry Reynolds,
Esquire, of Poets and Poesie.*
[5] *Gabriel Harvey's Marginalia*, ed. G. C. Moore-Smith (1913), 231.

and resplendent abiliments'.[1] This list is significant; Meres is giving a considered judgement of the most notable English poets of his day. Warner is included and with him Sir Philip Sidney, Spenser, Daniel, Drayton, Shakespeare, Marlow and Chapman. This is a splendid company. Later he considers Warner himself.

As Decius Ausonius Gallus, *in libris Fastorum*, penned the occurrences of the world from the first creation of it to his time . . . so Warner in his absolute *Albions England* hath most admirably penned the historie of his own country from Noah to his time, that is, to the raigne of Quenne Elizabeth; I have heard him termed of the best wits of both our Universities, our English Homer. As Euripedes is the most sententious among the Greek poets: so is Warner among our English poets.[2]

It may be doubted how much even the best wits of the universities knew of Homer, though the study of Greek was quite firmly established by then and the two poets which Professors of Greek were required to lecture on were Homer and Euripides. The first edition of Homer in Greek published in England (and the last for sixty-nine years) had come out seven years before. More important, the first seven books of Chapman's translation appeared in the same year. But to most of the wits Homer probably still meant what he had meant to Dante, and I do not suppose that Meres's encomium showed much more than that he was regarded as the leading English writer of history in verse. The comparison with Euripides, however, was more significant.

In 1600, two years after the *Palladis Tamia*, Robert Allott

---

[1] *Elizabethan Critical Essays*, II, 315. (Meres's list of Greek and Roman poets is one that could be accepted with few changes today: Homer, Hesiod, Euripides, Aeschylus, Sophocles, Pindar, Phocylides and Aristophanes; Virgil, Ovid, Horace, Silius Italicus, Lucan, Lucretius, Ausonius and Claudian. A little later Meres speaks of Warner with Sidney, Spenser, Daniel, Drayton and Shakespeare. *Op. cit.*, II, 318).

[2] *Op. cit.*, II, 317.

edited an anthology of the 'choysest Flowers of our Moderne Poets', containing no fewer than 2350 extracts.[1] No doubt allowance must be made for the editor's personal predilections, but it has every appearance of being a popular book. I think its modern editor is justified in claiming that 'its great merits are that it is an epitome of the influential poetry of the time, and that it enables us to form a fairly accurate opinion of the estimation in which the poets of the age were held by their contemporaries'. We find 387 extracts from Spenser and 226 from Drayton; Warner comes next with 171. Eighth place is taken by Shapespeare with 95. Still, we must not make too much of Robert Allott's preferences. Another anthologist of the time, John Bodenham, produced a book called *Belvedere* with no fewer than 4482 extracts, though most were of single lines and none more than couplets. He never once quoted Warner. More significant is the choice which Allott made from *Albions England*.

The title-page of *Englands Parnassus* claims that it contains 'Descriptions of Bewties, Personages, Castles, Pallaces, Mountaines, groves, Seas, Springs, Rivers &c. Whereunto are annexed other various discourses, both pleasant and profitable'. This gives a very false idea of the collection. It was 'discourses, both pleasant and profitable' which interested the editor, and a very fair description of the book can be gained from this extract from 'A Table of all the speciall matters contained in this Booke', Tasting, Teares, Temperance, Thoughts, Thetis, Time, Truth, Theologie, Treason, Trees, Tyrannie, Thirst, Tempests. These thirteen 'speciall matters' provide sixty-seven extracts, but of these only one came under the heading, Trees, and nine under Tempests. Allott was seeking for aphorisms and it was these he found in such abundance in Warner's poem. Only six of the extracts from *Albions England* are of more than six lines. What he admired in Warner was obviously that he was sententious — like Euripides. And in our eyes this is Warner at his worst.

[1] Robert Allott, *Englands Parnassus*, ed. C. Crawford (Oxford, 1913).

Full soone the fairest face would cease from being such,
If not preserved curiously from tending more than much,

or

We think no greater blisse, than such to be, as be we would,
When blessed none, but such as he, the same, as be they
    should,

or (perhaps a little more successful),

It is a common point whereon the aged grosly runne,
Once to have dared said & seene, more than was ever done.

A remarkable number of the extracts come from Warner's unfortunate essay in Philosophy.

A critic towards the end of the seventeenth century was to speak of Warner as 'a good honest plain writer of Moral rules and precepts'.[1] Warner's sententiousness obviously meant a great deal to his contemporaries. We shall not share their appreciation of it. But it is very rare for us to be impressed by the aphorisms of our forebears. Nothing in literature loses its savour more quickly.

However, the poem was admired for more than its precepts. 'As Homer and Virgil among the Greeks and Latines are the chief Heroick poets,' wrote Meres, 'so Spencer and Warner be our chiefe heroicall makers,'[2] and the Earl of Essex spoke of the 'diverse notable pageants' in *Albions England*, holding that nowhere were English and other histories 'more sensibly described, or more inwardly discovered'.[3] Warner stands or falls as a story-teller.

He had a new story to tell and many old ones. The new story was the history of his own country. An Englishman, in the days when Warner brought out the early editions of his poem, could find this history, complete from the days of Brutus to his own, in the Chronicles from Higden, through Fabyan and Stow, to Holinshed, published nine years before *Albions*

[1] Edward Phillips, *Theatrum Poetarum* (1675), quoted in W. Warner, *Syrinx*, ed. W. A. Bacon, xxii.
[2] *Elizabethan Critical Essays*, II, 319.
[3] *Gabriel Harvey's Marginalia*, 232.

England. For twenty years before Holinshed the popularity of
The Mirrour for Magistrates had shown that Englishmen felt
that their country's history had in it the material for poetry.
But the *Mirrour* was not a history; it left out far too much.
Warner combined in one book two very popular traditions; in
it there is found together the sweep of Holinshed and the liking
for a good story to be found in the *Mirrour*.

He had set himself a hard task. Warner was a genuine
historian. The most original feature of his book is that he was
more interested in the earlier part of his history, that of England
under the Anglo-Saxons, Normans and Plantagenets, than he
was in the Wars of the Roses. Like a true historian he found
historical facts exciting in themselves; he delighted in a family
tree. But he was well aware that his readers might not share his
interest. For him the Normans were an intrusion and the
marriage of Henry I to an English princess was an event of deep
significance. It set his mind travelling down a long and glorious
genealogical table. But he knew this could hardly make a poem.

> With Hengests blood our droupen Muse it also now revives
> For harshly sounds our Poeme save in matter where it
>   thrives.
> Let be your bitten Vine, we here a blisfull Vintage gaine,
> That did, and doth, and evermore unblasted may remaine:
> For this corivall seed begot England English againe.
> From whence we note what Scepters, what discents, &
>   turnes befel:
> Lesse pleasing unto some, perhaps, then toyes which many
>   tell,
> That but of phansies, women, loves, and wantonnes can sing:
> From which their tunes: but pipp their tongs & then they
>   hang the wing.[1]

So he livened his history with such 'toyes', writing, as Chettle
said, 'sweete mixt layes of majestie with mirth.' Some of these
stories were drawn from classical mythology, and there too he
knew his public. It is difficult for us to share the delight which

[1] Book V, Chapter 22, p. 114.

the Elizabethan Englishman found in these tales. The Renaissance brought a new discovery of the world of Greek and Latin
stories; but it was as if a country, every inch of which was
known, was suddenly explored all over again and found to be
new. There was nothing scholarly about the exploration.
Consider those amazing lines from Faustus's apostrophe to
Helen in Marlowe's play,

> More lovely than the monarch of the sky
> In wanton Arethusa's azur'd arms.

The beautiful Helena compared with the bearded Jupiter,
dallying with a maiden of whom there is not a line of evidence
in classical literature that he ever met her at all. What could
be more absurd, and what more triumphantly successful? It
would be ridiculous to compare Warner with Marlowe at his
most splendid, but he too, when he turned to the myths of
Greece and Rome, found in them an intoxicating freshness and
delight.

   Warner's stories were not all drawn from classical mythology:
some were English enough and some seem to have been his own.
Let me conclude with one which alone kept his name alive
through the succeeding generations, the 'Storie of Curan and
Argentile'.[1] It was pirated by the sellers of broadsheets and was
used by a seventeenth-century dramatist for his plot; in 1765
it was reprinted by Bishop Percy. William Mason, the friend
and editor of Thomas Gray, would speak of the lady whom he
was to marry as his Argentile and he wrote a play himself
based on the story.

> The Brutons thus departed hence, Seaven Kingdomes here
>   begonne:
> Where diversly in divers broyles the Saxons lost and wonne.
> King Edel and King Adelbright in Diria jointly raigne,
> In loyall concorde during life these Kingly friends remaine.

King Adelbright dies and on his deathbed urges his brother,
Edel, to bring up his daughter, Argentile, and when she was
grown up, to resign to her the throne.

[1] Book IV, Chapter 20, pp. 93–8.

Curan, 'Sonne unto a Prince in Danske', visits Edel's court, sees Argentile and falls in love with her. Finding that no nobleman is 'admitted to her vewe', he becomes a 'Kitchin Drudge',

> That so at least of life or death she might become his Judge.
> Accesse so had to see, and speake, he did his love bewray,
> And tels his birth: her answer was she husbandles would stay.

The king, however, decides that the best way to get rid of Argentile is to marry her off to some peasant and he picks on Curan as a suitable husband. Argentile indignantly rejects the king's proposal and flees the court; Curan in despair departs also. He becomes a shepherd and gradually, as two years pass, his love for Argentile grows fainter and he falls in love with a Neatherd's maid.

> A countrie wench, a Neatherds maid, where Curan kept his
>   sheep,
> Did feed her Drove: and now on her was all the
>   Shepheards keepe:
> He borrowed on the working daies his holy russets oft,
> And of the bacons fat, to make his Startopes blacke and soft,
> And least his Tarbox should offend, he left it at the Fold,
> Sweete Growte, or whig, his bottle had as much as it might
>   hold,
> A Sheeve of bread as browne as Nut, and Cheese as white as
>   snow,
> And wildings, or the Seasons-fruit he did in scrip bestow,
> And whil'st his py-bald Curre did sleepe, & sheep-hooke
>   lay him by,
> On hollow Quilles of Oaten straw he piped melody:
> But when he spied her his Saint, he wipte his greasie
>   shooes,
> And clear'd the drivel from his beard and thus the
>   Shepherd wooes.

He urges the claims of a shepherd as a lover.

> The Plowmans labour hath no end, and he a Churle will
>   prove:

The Craftsman hath more worke in hand then fitted unto
    love:
The Marchant, traffiquing abroad, suspects his wife at
    home:
A youth will play the wanton, and an old man proove a
    Mome:
Then chuse a Shepheard: with the Sun he doth his Flocke
    unfold,
And all the day on Hill or Plaine he merrie chat can hold,
And with the Sun doth folde againe: then jogging home
    betime,
He turnes a Crab, or tunes a round, or sings some merrie
    ryme:
Nor lacks he gleeful tales, whil'st round the nut-brown bole
    doth trot,
And sitteth singing care-away, till he to bed be got:
There sleepes he soundly all the night, forgetting Morrow
    cares,
Nor feares he blasting of his Corne nor uttering of his wares,
Or stormes by seas, or stirres of land, or cracke of credit lost,
Not spending franklier than his Flocke shall still defray the
    cost:
Well wot I, sooth they say that say more quiet night and
    daies
The Shepheard sleeps & wakes then he whose Cattel he doth
    graze.

Here the story takes an unexpected turn. Curan continues,

Beleeve me, Lasse, a King is but a man, and so am I:
Content is worth a Monarchie, and mischiefes hit the hie,
As late it did a King and his, not dwelling farre from hence,
Who left a Daughter, (save thy selfe) for faire a matchlesse
    wench:
(Here did he pause, as if his tongue had done his heart
    offence.)

The shepherdess urges him to say more about this lady.
Curan's description turns out in the end to be more than just
one of those catalogues of a mistress's beauties, which can be

found countless times in Elizabethan poetry. While he begins
with an eye still on the girl he is now courting, he gradually
forgets her as his mind is recalled to the Argentile he is
deserting.

> The Neatresse, longing for the rest, did egge him on to tell
> How faire she was, and who she was. She bore (quoth he) the
>   bell
> For Beautie: though I clownish am, I know what Beautie is,
> Or did I not, yet seeing thee, I senseles were to mis.
> Suppose her Beautie Hellens-like, or Hellens somewhat less:
> And every Starre consorting to a pure Complexion gesse:
> Her stature comely, tall, her gate well graced, and her wit
> To marvell at, nor meddle with, as matchles I omit:
> A Globe-like head, a Gold-like haire, a Forhead smooth and
>   hie,
> An even Nose, on either side did shine a grayish Eie:
> Two rosie Cheekes, round ruddy Lips, white just-set
>   Teeth within:
> A mouth in meane, and underneath a round and dimpled
>   Chin:

I need not complete the Catalogue and let these two lines
suffice,

> And more, her long and limber armes had white and azure
>   wrists,
> And slender Fingers answere to her smooth and lillie Fists:
> A legge in Print, a pretie Foot. . . .

He ends at last,

> Her smiles were sober, and her lookes were chearefull unto all,
> Even such as neither wanton seeme, nor waiward, mell, nor
>   gall:
> A quiet minde, a patient mood, and not disdaining any:
> Not gibing, gadding, gawdy, and sweete faculties had many.
> A Nimph, no tong, no heart, no eie, might praise, might
>   wish, might see,
> For life, for love, for forme, more good, more worth, more
>   fair then she,

Yea such an one, as such was none, save onely she was such:
Of Argentile to say the most were to be silent much.

The ending of the story is unexpected and absurd, but something more.

I knew the Lady very well, but worthles of such praies,
The Neatresse said: and muse I do, a Shepheard thus
    should blaze
The Coote of Beautie: Credit me, thy latter speech bewraies
Thy clownish shape a coined shew. But wherefore doest
    thou weepe?
(The Shepheard wept, and she was woe, and both doth
    silence keepe.)
In troth, quoth he, I am not such as seeming I professe,
But then for her, and now for thee I from my selfe digresse:
Her loved I, (wretch that I am a Recreant to be)
I loved her that hated love, but now I die for thee.
At Kirkland is my Fathers Court, and Curan is my name,
In Edels Court sometimes in pompe, till love contrould the
    same:
But now. What now? dear hart, how now? what ailest thou
    to weep?
(The Damsell wept, and he was woe, and both did silence
    keepe.)
I graunt, quoth she, it was too much, that you did love so
    much:
But whom your former could not move, your second love
    doth touch.
Thy twise beloved Argentile submiteth her to thee,
And for thy double love presents her selfe a single free,
In passing, not in person chaung'd, and I, my Lord, am she.
They sweetely surfeiting in joy, and silent for a space,
When as the Extasie had end did tenderly imbrace,
And for their wedding and their wish got fitting time and
    place.

Warner surely in this story has risen above the level of the
ballad tale. Those 'silences which both did keep' give it a
strangely realistic note. It no longer seems to us quite absurd.

If Warner was admired in his own day, he can at least tell us something about its interests and points of view. But is he more than a piece of historical evidence? I think he is. No one could claim that he was more than a minor poet. He attempted the impossible. No one could have written a convincing long poem in fourteeners, as Chapman found when he translated Homer. But he abandoned them when he came to the *Odyssey*, and Warner could hardly do that. But read, not as an epic, but in separate chapters, I think we can often find pleasure in his poem, as Charles Lamb did. Warner must have meant it to be read in that way. Many of his chapters end with a 'to be continued in our next', which makes his intention clear enough.

But a more searching question is, Do we enjoy him merely because he is quaint? No doubt he often is. His naivety, his very incompetence, the alliterations (though these are not so very frequent) and antitheses, which delighted Lamb, give us something of the amusement we find in children. But I believe we can find something more. As long as we do not read too much of his poem at a stretch (for, if we do, 'the lagging fourteener' will certainly be too much for us), we should be able to recapture something of his unjaded interest in the history of his country. And, further, there are times when Warner gives us that particular delight which we can derive from a primitive writer who is a genuine poet, or a primitive painter who is a genuine artist. We feel the urge to express depths and subtleties, which had been beyond the range of their contemporaries, struggling against the lack of experience in their technique. This can move us more than the titillation of mere quaintness, and Warner, to my mind, sometimes moves us in that way.

II

Nathaniel Lee
The Rival Queens

RESTORATION Tragedy, of all the great traditions in English literature, is the one that is most disliked. It is not ignored — Dryden makes that impossible; it is not disapproved of on moral grounds as Restoration Comedy often is; it is regarded as distasteful. Bombast, rant, mechanical plots, threadbare stage devices, such words and phrases are found in almost every history of English literature. Above all, it is considered false. Only a few weeks ago a review in *The Times Literary Supplement* of Professor Bonamy Dobrée's recent collection of *Five Heroic Plays* summed it all up by declaring that 'these plays, though, no doubt, a fact of literary history, are an insult to human integrity'.

Nathaniel Lee, about one of whose plays I shall be speaking to-day, was regarded by his contemporaries as one of their foremost tragic dramatists. We are more likely to approach him with caution, if not with an actual prejudice against him. Literary histories will have led us to expect him to be one of the worst of a bad lot. Some consideration of the school of dramatic writing to which he belonged seems desirable before we look at his play *The Rival Queens*.

When reading English critics of Restoration Tragedy, I am constantly reminded of the ordinary Englishman's reaction to the Baroque churches and to the paintings and statuary in them, which he sees when he visits South Germany or Austria. To him they seem, above all, irreligious. All that mass of painted stucco, the violently dramatised figures flanking the altars, the swirling angels soaring above on the painted ceilings, the cherubic orchestras perched on the organ screens with absurd little putti playing 'cellos they can hardly reach round or whanging away on kettle-drums — they may be thought decorative, but they are obviously unspiritual. To one who sees in the altar figures personifications in the drama of the great conflicts between good and evil in the human soul and in human society, for whom the ceiling paintings are superb attempts to bridge the gulf between the Church Militant below and the saints in Heaven above, who looks on the playing putti as expressing the dedication by man to God of all that is absurd and laughable on earth, these criticisms are quite baffling. There seems to be no point of contact. However, as there are some signs that in recent years Baroque painting, unlike Restoration Tragedy, is becoming rather less distasteful to Englishmen, we might, perhaps, see whether painting can help us and turn to Dryden's *Parallel of Poetry and Painting*, which he prefixed to his translation in 1695 of du Fresnoy's *De Arte Graphica*.[1]

Dryden begins with a long extract from the *Lives of the Painters and Sculptors* by Giovanni Pietro Bellori. Bellori had expounded the Platonic view, conventional in his day, that it was the duty of the painter to depict ideal beauty, not the deformed and disproportioned forms he will find in the sublunary world. 'The artful painter and the sculptor, imitating the Divine Maker, form to themselves, as well as they are able, a model of the superior beauties; and reflecting on them, endeavour to correct and amend the common nature, and to represent it as it was first created, without fault, either in colour or in lineament.' Quoting from Maximus Tyrius, Bellori had said that 'the image which is taken by the painter from several bodies produces a beauty which it is impossible to find in any single natural body, approaching to the perfection of the fairest statues. Thus nature on this account is much inferior to art'. And so, Bellori had concluded, 'the fancy more persuades the painter than the imitation; for the last makes only the things which it sees, but the first makes also the things which it never sees.'

[1] *Essays of John Dryden*, ed. W. P. Ker (Oxford, 1926), II, 115–153.

Dryden was well aware that the dramatist's task was not quite that of the painter and that he had other work to do than to portray perfect beauty. It would be impossible to create dramatic situations out of perfect beings. 'The perfection of stage-characters,' he says, 'consists chiefly in their likeness to the deficient faulty nature, which is their original.' We must not misunderstand this statement and think that Dryden meant that a dramatist should portray men and women as they actually are, with all their complexities of strength and weakness, nobility and meanness. It is true that he says that 'to imitate Nature well in whatsoever subject is the perfection of both arts', that is, the arts of painting and poetry, including drama. But Dryden was very far from advocating a drama which was 'true to life'.

> Since a true knowledge of Nature gives us pleasure, a lively imitation of it, either in Poetry or Painting, must of necessity produce a much greater: for both these arts, as I said before, are not only true imitations of Nature, but of the best Nature, of that which is wrought up to a nobler pitch. They present us with images more perfect than the life in any individual [by 'perfect' he did not mean 'morally perfect']: and we have the pleasure to see all the scattered beauties of Nature united by a happy chemistry, without its deformities or faults.

The dramatic artist, then, is true to nature when his characters, although in one sense 'impossible', are compounded of actual human qualities. Dramatic chemistry needs realistic ingredients.

At one point in this essay Dryden refers to his own play *All for Love*.

> My characters of Antony and Cleopatra, though they are favourable to them, have nothing of outrageous panegyric. Their passions were their own, and such as were given them by history; only the deformities of them were cast into shadows, that they might be objects of compassion: whereas if I had chosen a noon-day light for them, somewhat must have been discovered which would rather have moved our hatred than our pity.

The over-riding factor in the writing of a play was not the creation of characters, but the framing of the whole play. If in a play a shadow is cast so that certain characteristics of a person are obscured, the dramatist will obviously not be producing a realistic character, but he may feel it necessary to do this in order to preserve the artistic purpose of the play.

Bellori's theory of painting and the use made of it by Dryden when discussing poetry and the drama should help us to understand the Tragedies of Dryden's — and of Nathaniel Lee's — time, and give us a clue to the particular characteristic of their plays which leads so many to think that they are fundamentally false. To accuse Nathaniel Lee of creating, in the play we shall consider, an Alexander the Great or two rival queens, Statira and Roxana, who were impossible characters, because there never was or could be an Alexander, a Statira, or a Roxana like them, would be to mistake his intention. This was not to create actual human beings, but a man, in Alexander, who was, as it were, compacted of many heroes, and two rivals who might be said to sum up two very different types of women. In fact, I think he would have claimed that the drama demanded this, because the tension of the dramatic situation would be the greater if the two rivals were wholly opposite to one another in character. The business of the play for him would be to create one overwhelming thunder-clap, not a prolonged rumble of distant thunder-clouds, unable, as it were, to get to grips with one another, which is what happens in real life where individuals are part one thing, part another, constantly ready for the compromises which dissolve a dramatic situation.

Bellori, referring to a passage in the *Timaeus*, had said, 'If you take a man as he is made by nature, and compare him with another, who is an effect of art, the work of nature will always appear less beautiful, because art is more accurate than nature.' And Lee might claim that these idealised figures would indeed be more accurate than nature, more accurate to that ideal figure of the conquering hero or the wronged wife or mistress, which alone makes possible at all the existence of the sublunary heroes or jealous ladies whom we meet in our ordinary lives.

If we can see what the authors of the Restoration Tragedies were trying to do, we may find it easier to have some respect for their integrity. It is naturally difficult for us to appreciate them, because we live in an age which delights in exploring the complexities of human nature. Quite apart from the psychologist of recent times, we have behind us the development of the Novel, a form of literature as perfectly adapted to the exploration of the human personality as the drama is to its formal presentation. I should say that the best commentary on our contemporary attitude towards the Heroic Drama is to be found in an opera, the *Ariadne auf Naxos* of Richard Strauss. Ariadne and Zerbinetta cannot be reconciled, and in the end it is Bacchus and Ariadne, not Arlecchino and Zerbinetta, who hold the stage.

Some attempt to compare the influence on Restoration Tragedy of the French drama of the time and the earlier English drama of the Jacobean and Carolean days would be necessary in any complete study of Lee's plays, but this cannot be undertaken now. I should draw attention, however, to the influence of Beaumont and Fletcher, which Lee himself acknowledged. Their plays made dramatists seek for the creation of particular dramatic situations, which would enable them to depict in the strongest light the conflict of passions. This might easily become meretricious; it was only too easy to turn a play into a means of bringing two opposing characters into conflict with one another and then of allowing them to exploit the situations rhetorically. It may have been the traditions of the Carolean stage, lasting over the Commonwealth period, which had produced actors trained to do this. Certainly, once they were there, such actors demanded plays which would give them the opportunity to display their particular talents. We must not forget that in the 1670's, when Lee was writing, there were only two theatres in London. An author was forced to provide the kind of play the companies wanted, and that meant one considered suitable for a mere handful of actors and actresses. The tradition of acting to-day is an altogether different one and we are likely to find it almost impossible to imagine how some of the scenes and speeches in Restoration Tragedy could have been successful.

Once more, we are liable to think that they are false, lacking in integrity, and once more we should consider what the dramatists were trying to do. Dryden in his *Essay of Dramatic Poesy*, written in 1668, had defended stoutly the use of the rhymed couplet and his defence had really covered the whole tradition of the poetic diction used in the tragedies of his day. He summed up his arguments in his *Defence of the Essay*, which followed a few months later.

> 'Tis true, that to imitate well is a poet's work; but to affect the soul, and excite the passions, and, above all, to move admiration (which is the delight of serious plays), a bare imitation will not serve. The converse, therefore, which a poet is to imitate, must be heightened with all the arts and ornaments of poesy; and must be such as, strictly considered, could never be supposed spoken by any without premeditation.[1]

The language of the dramatists of Dryden's time can often be criticised, but it should not be criticised for not doing what it did not intend to do. The opponent of rhymed verse in Dryden's *Essay* had asked, 'what is more unbefitting the majesty of verse, than to call a servant, or bid a door be shut in rhyme?' In reply Neander (that is Dryden himself) had said that Seneca had shown that one could make such a remark 'sound high and lofty', when he wrote '*Reserate clusos regii postes laris*'. In the second edition of his *Essay* Dryden added a translation, 'Set wide the palace gates.' By doing this he gave the show away, for it is one thing to say 'unlock the door' and quite another to say 'set wide the gates'. He was on surer ground when he suggested that 'such thoughts should be waved, as often as may be, by the address of the poet'.[2] It was not the business of the dramatist to have his characters calling servants or unlocking doors, but to place them in situations where noble verse seemed appropriate. Again, I think we must allow a great deal for the

[1] *Essays of John Dryden*, I, 113–14.   [2] *Ibid.*, I, 93, 104–5.

demands of the actors. There have been and are actors who
can produce a great effect by calling a servant or unlocking a
door — but not Henry Betterton or Mrs Barry. But they could
declaim 'Set wide the palace gates' in a way which would keep
quiet even the intolerably unruly audiences of the Restoration
theatres.

The Rival Queens is sometimes taken as a perfect example
of Restoration Tragedy at its most absurd. But we have to
account for the fact that on the stage it was extremely popular,
not only in its own day, but for the next hundred and fifty
years. The greatest actors and actresses played in it, from
Betterton to Charles Kemble and Edmund Kean, from Mrs
Barry to Mrs Siddons. It was revived by Kean as late as 1823
and only after that disappeared from the stage. It was continually reprinted until 1815. In 1745 Horace Walpole showed
where he placed Lee when he wrote, 'I cannot bear modern
poetry; these refiners of the purity of the stage, and of the
incorrectness of English verse, are most wofully insipid. I had
rather have written the most absurd lines in Lee, than *Leonidas*
or *The Seasons*.' But more than forty years later he said that the
part in which he really wanted to see Mrs Siddons was in one of
Lee's plays.[1]

Nathaniel Lee was born about 1648. His father, William Lee,
was a London clergyman, then Chaplain to General Monk, and,
after the Restoration, Vicar of Hatfield. He was a man of some
standing and frequently preached at Court. Nathaniel was
nominated to Charterhouse in 1658 and in 1665 went up to
Trinity College, Cambridge, becoming a B.A. in 1669. It is said
that 'at college he was eccentric, but sedulous and ambitious'.[2]
A year later a poem of his was included in the tribute paid by
Cambridge University to George Monk, Duke of Albemarle, on
his death. He seems to have been taken up by the Duke of
Buckingham, who soon dropped him, after which he went up to

[1] *Letters of Horace Walpole*, ed. Mrs Paget Toynbee (1903–5), II,
82 (29 March 1745); XIV, 42 (15 January 1788).

[2] Samuel Dunham, *Lives of the most Eminent Literary Men of Great
Britain* (1838), III, 135.

London and early in 1673 played the part of Duncan in D'Avenant's operatic version of *Macbeth*. He suffered from stage-fright and had to abandon the career of an actor. Perhaps his short experience on the stage and the fact that he was regarded as a superlatively good reader of plays may account for his ability to write exactly the kind of drama the leading actors and actresses of the time wanted. He became a playwright and his first play, *The Tragedy of Nero*, was produced at the Drury Lane Theatre in May 1674.

His literary career was a short one. He wrote altogether eleven plays and twice collaborated with Dryden. He was, to begin with, a strong supporter of the Whigs and his tragedy, *Lucius Junius Brutus*, was promptly suppressed in December 1680. It is well worth reading, not only as a fine play, but also for its exposition of Whig political theories. However, he later moved over to the Tory side; it was generally supposed under Dryden's influence. All his plays were tragedies and the themes were always historical, either from Greek or Roman history or from the century before his own. *The Rival Queens* was first produced in March 1679, his last play in 1683. In November 1684 he was confined in Bedlam.

The accounts of Nathaniel Lee's lunacy are horrible. Later gossip-writers gave him a reputation for drunkenness, but there is nothing to show that he was more dissolute than most others in the circle of the Court and the Theatre in Charles II's reign, and his plays are a great deal freer of indecency than those of most other contemporary playwrights. He had been for a decade one of the most successful dramatists of the time. Now he was to achieve a new notoriety which quite obscured his literary renown. He became an object for sightseers. Wycherley wrote ghoulishly of his being starved and whipped by his keepers. Stories were told linking his madness with his writings. It was said that he had written, while in Bedlam, a play of twenty-five acts, that 'while he was writing one of his scenes by moonlight, a cloud intervening, he cried out in ecstacy, "Jove snuff the Moon" ' and that he told someone who visited him of a couplet he had written,

I've seen an Unscrew'd spider spin a thought,
And walk away upon the wings of angells![1]

He became known as Mad Nat Lee, and the plays which he had
written came to be regarded as the exercises of a madman.

In 1689 he was discharged from Bedlam — one wonders how
a madman ever recovered in that place — and he is said to have
been granted a pension of £10 a year.[2] One of his plays, *The
Princess of Cleves*, was performed again and then disappeared
for good from the stage. A performance before Queen Mary of
The Massacre of Paris, known as the Protestant Play and very
suitable for an age which had seen the departure of James II,
was more successful, drawing tears from the audience. Colley
Cibber remembered him coming each week to the Theatre
Royal to draw his pension.[3] And then, early in May 1692,
'returning one night late from the Bear and Harrow tavern in
Butcher Row, thro close market to his lodgings in Duke Street
overladen with wine, he fell down on the ground some say
(according to others on a bulk) and was chilled or stifled in the
snow and was found dead.'[4]

Within three years of his death Dryden, who had been his
friend and had twice collaborated with him (one of the plays,
Oedipus, being a very great success, of which Dryden was always
proud), wrote of him as one who, though he 'had a great genius
for Tragedy, following the fury of his natural temper, made every
man, and woman too, in his plays, stark raging mad; there
was not a sober person to be had for love or money'.[5] The
exaggeration is absurd, but it was remembered. In his last
plays, when there is no doubt that he saw his own madness
coming on him, there are indeed constant references to the
theme. It is significant that in one of these, *Caesar Borgia*, he
gives a picture of madness which is frighteningly convincing.

[1] R. G. Ham, *Otway and Lee* (New Haven, 1931), 210.
[2] Article on Nathaniel Lee in *D.N.B.* by Sir Sidney Lee.
[3] *The Works of Nathaniel Lee*, ed. T. B. Stroup and A. L. Cooke
(New Brunswick, 1955), I, 17.
[4] MS note by William Oldys, quoted in R. G. Ham, *op. cit.*, 219.
[5] *Essays of John Dryden*, II, 142.

Probably only someone who was on the verge of madness could have written it.

Having established that all his characters were mad, Dryden went on, 'All was tempestuous and blustering; heaven and earth were coming together at every word; a mere hurricane from the beginning to the end, and every actor seemed to be hastening on the day of judgment.' No doubt Dryden forgot that in the preface which he had written for *The Rival Queens* he had said,

> They only think you animate your theme
> With too much fire, who are themselves all phlegm.

However, Dryden's words, 'tempestuous and blustering', are the usual picture that is given of Lee's plays. They became a by-word, 'the furious fustian and turgid rants of Nat Lee's *Alexander the Great*,' as Colley Cibber put it in his *Apology*. 'If you would see Passion in its purity, without admixture of Reason,' wrote Steele in a rather prim essay in *The Spectator* on keeping one's temper, 'behold it represented in a mad Hero, drawn by a mad poet.'[1] He was referring to Alexander in *The Rival Queens*. But Alexander in this play is not mad and the very rhetorical lines which Steele then quoted to prove his point were in fact not spoken by Alexander at all, but by a jealous woman, distraught at losing the affections of her husband.

It would be pointless to deny that Lee rants; the mistake is to think he does nothing else. It is easy to remember the ranting and to disregard the lines that show he could be a poet. I should say that the worst lines he ever wrote — and the competition is severe — come in his play *Lucius Junius Brutus*, when Sempronia, Brutus's wife, brings their young son to plead for his brother who is condemned to death.

> His pretty eyes ruddy and wet with tears,
> Like two burst Cherries rowling in a storm,
> Plead for our griefs more than a thousand Tongues.[2]

But the play as a whole does not make at all a ridiculous impression. Far more typical of its general tone are the splendid and dignified words of Brutus with which it closes. I can think

---

[1] *The Spectator*, No. 438 (23 July, 1712).   [2] *Op. cit.*, V, ii, 100–3.

D

of no finer concluding lines of any English tragedy, including
Shakespeare's, especially the last resounding couplet.

> Let Heav'n and Earth for ever keep their bound,
> The Stars unshaken go their constant Round;
> In harmless labour be our steel employ'd,
> And endless peace thro all the World enjoy'd:
> Let every Bark the Waves in safety Plough,
> No angry Tempest curl the Ocean's brow;
> No darted flames from Heav'n make Mortals fear,
> Nor Thunder fright the weeping Passenger;
> Let not poor Swains for Storms at Harvest mourn,
> But smile to see their hoards of bladed Corn:
> No dreadful Comets threaten from the Skies,
> No Venom fall, nor poys'nous Vapours rise.
> Thou, Jove, who dost the Fates of Empires Doom,
> Guard, and Defend the Liberty of Rome.[1]

Before I come to consider *The Rival Queens* I should say a
word on its sources. Lee owed something, though not as much
as is generally suggested, to a novel, la Calprenède's *Cassandre*.
But the rivalry between Roxana and Statira was derived from
Plutarch and he also used Quintus Curtius, occasionally almost
translating him.[2] These two authors embodied in their lives
of Alexander two contradictory traditions, the one showing him
as a strong, self-disciplined man of action, the other as one
ruined by success, who became a tyrant and a drunkard. Lee
succeeded in combining these two traditions in such a way as
to make of Alexander a more complex character than was often
found in the Heroic Drama. But Lee did not depend only on
the nature of his sources for this. In one of his characters in
another play, Caesar Borgia, he was to show again that he was
capable of depicting an internal dramatic conflict and not only
one produced by the meeting of two opposing characters.

A word of warning is needed about certain phrases and

[1] *Op. cit.*, V, ii, 197–210.

[2] Gerard Langbaine in his *Account of the English Dramatick Poets*,
(Oxford, 1691), 325, said that Lee also consulted Arrian, Justin,
Diodorus Siculus and Josephus, but this seems to me very doubtful.

sentences in the play. This is a danger that faces every poet. Some line or phrase, through no fault of his, but simply owing to a change in the meaning of a word or some new formed association of two words, or because it can be given a satirical twist by an irreverent reader, simply goes bad. There is a perfect instance in this play, the line in a speech by one of the Queens about Alexander,

> Then he would talk, good Gods, how he would talk!

Once the line is isolated and its satirical possibilities are recognised, there is nothing that can save it. Professor Bonamy Dobrée, I think rather wickedly, puts it at the head of the chapter on Nathaniel Lee in his *Restoration Tragedy*. But it did not give that impression to his contemporaries. Addison, in a passage in *The Spectator* which is critical of Lee for his 'clouds of words', refers to it, as follows:

> He frequently succeeds in the passionate parts of the Tragedy, but more particularly where he slackens his efforts and eases the stile of those epithets and metaphors, in which he so much abounds. What can be more natural, more soft or more passionate than that line in Statira's speech, where she describes the charm of Alexander's conversation?

> Then he would talk, good Gods, how he would talk! That unexpected break in the line and turning the description of his manner of talking into an admiration of it, is inexpressibly beautiful and wonderfully suited to the fond character of the person who speaks it. There is a simplicity in the words that outshines the utmost power of expression.[1]

But some sixty years later Dr Johnson, writing to Mrs Thrale, said,

> Tom Lisgow is an assembly. But Tom Lisgow cannot people the world. Mr K—— must have a place. The lion has its jackall. They will soon meet.

> And when they talk, ye gods! how they will talk. Pray let your voice and my master's help to fill the pauses.[2]

[1] *The Spectator*, No. 39 (14 April, 1711).
[2] *Letters of Samuel Johnson*, ed. G. B. Hill (1892), Johnson to Mrs Thrale, 19 February 1773, I, 207.

At some time during the interval the ridiculous interpretation of the line must have become apparent to someone; the harm once done, nothing could ever save the line again.

We are only too likely to find such lines in a play by Nathaniel Lee. I feel that we should do what we can to avoid putting our own interpretation on them, but it may well be impossible. At one point in the play one of the Rival Queens says of Alexander,

> I know he's false;
> 'Tis now the common talk, the news of the world.

We are pretty well helpless in face of that. The detachment necessary when reading such phrases can be much more difficult to achieve than that willing suspension of disbelief which Coleridge demanded of us when we read a poem.

The scene of *The Rival Queens*, we are told, is Babylon. It opens violently, 'Enter Hephestion, Lysimachus, fighting: Clytus parting them.'

> *Clytus:* What, are you Mad-men! Ha Put up I say
>   Then, mischief in the bosoms of ye both.
> *Lysimachus:* I have his Sword.
> *Clytus:*   But must not have his Life.
> *Lysimachus:* Must not Old Clytus?
> *Clytus:* Mad Lysimachus, you must not.[1]

Clytus having separated them begins the business of informing the audience of the situation when the play begins, and also of introducing them to one of its main themes, the contrast between Alexander the World Conqueror and the Alexander who is Love's slave.

> And what's the noble Cause that makes this madness?
> What big Ambition blows this dangerous Fire?
> A Cupids puff, is it not Woman's breath?
> By all your triumphs in the heat of Youth,
> When Towns were sack'd, and Beauties prostrate lay,
> When my Blood boil'd and Nature work'd me high,
> Clytus ne're bow'd his body to such shame:

---

[1] I, i, 1–5. (The text used, from *The Works of Nathaniel Lee*, ed. T. B. Stroup and A. L. Cooke, is that of the first Quarto of 1677.)

The brave will scorn their Cobweb Arts — The Souls
Of all that whining, smiling, coz'ning Sex
Weight not one thought of any Man of War.[1]

Lysimachus: I must confess our vengeance was ill-tim'd.

(Let us beware. That line may not have seemed faintly absurd
then, as it does now. This is an earlier use of the word 'ill-
timed' than is given in the New English Dictionary.)

Clytus: Death! I had rather this right Arm were lost,
   To which I owe my glory, than our King
   Should know your fault — what, on this famous day! . . .
                This memorable day,
   When our hot Master, that wou'd tire the World,
   Outride the lab'ring Sun and tread the Stars,
   When he inclin'd to rest, comes peaceful on,
   Listning to Songs: while all his Trumpets sleep,
   And plays with Monarchs whom he us'd to drive.[2]

Later Clytus again upbraids the two Captains for falling out
over a woman.

   O that a Face should thus bewitch a Soul,
   And ruine all that's right and reasonable.
   Talk be my bane, yet the Old Man must talk,
   Not so he lov'd when he at Issus fought;
   And join'd in mighty Duel great Darius,
   Whom from his Chariot flaming all with Gems
   He hurl'd to Earth and crush'd th' imperial Crown,
   Nor cou'd the Gods defend their Images
   Which with the gawdy Coach lay overturn'd:
   'Twas not the shaft of Love that did the feat,
   Cupid had nothing there to do, but now
   Two Wives he takes, two Rival Queens disturb
   The Court; and while each hand do's beauty hold,
   Where is their room for glory?
Hephestion: In his heart.
Clytus: Well said,
   You are his favourite, and I had forgot

---

[1] I, i, 27–36.   [2] I, i, 38–46.

Who I was talking to, see Sysigambis comes
Reading a Letter to your Princess; go,
Now make your claim, while I attend the King.[1]

And Clytus goes out.

As an opening scene this seems to me highly successful.
Clytus has introduced the main themes of the play, that of the
Rival Queens and the contrast between the two Alexanders.
Moreover, he has established himself and he is to perform a
most important function in the play as a kind of Chorus,
representing all the qualities that Alexander has forsaken. He
has, too, hinted at the grounds for the rivalry between Hephestion and Lysimachus, leaving these to be made clear in the
next scene. This rivalry is to be one of the two minor themes in
the play and was derived from la Calprenède's novel. It is far
from successfully handled and serves only to distract attention
from the main theme of the play.

Sysigambis, the mother of Darius, and Parisatis, Darius's
daughter, come in. She is imploring her grandmother to support
her in her love for Lysimachus. The two Captains plead their
cause and Sysigambis says that the question has already been
decided by Alexander's verdict in favour of Hephestion. The
two ladies leave, followed a moment after by the two Captains,
but before they go Hephestion notes the approach of Cassander.
Lysimachus says:

I wou'd avoid him,
There's something in that busie Face of his
That shocks my Nature.[2]

This is scanty preparation for Cassander, who is to be the
leading figure in another theme, taken from Curtius, a plot to
murder Alexander. It is, without doubt, the weakest element in
the play. For the next two hundred lines one is given the impression that it is to form the main theme, but, in fact, it is
subsequently for some time almost forgotten. It is so neglected
that it is hardly understandable and, as a result, the *dénouement*
of the play, which it eventually creates, seems quite purpose-

[1] I, i, 56–74.   [2] I, i, 129–31.

less. Lee, in fact, set himself an impossible task. The rivalry
between the two Queens and the portrayal of Alexander were
enough material for the play. It would have needed a much
surer hand than his to weld the story of a conspiracy which was
to cause Alexander's death into a coherent plot with the other
themes. Dryden might, perhaps, have managed it.

Cassander's opening soliloquy shows Lee at his worst, but if one
is to give a just idea of the play it can hardly be omitted. (The
part was taken by Edward Kynaston, a young actor just rising to
fame as a player of 'majestic' parts, and no doubt he enjoyed it.)

> The Morning rises black, the lowring Sun,
> As if the dreadful business he foreknew,
> Drives heavily his sable Chariot on:
> The Face of Day now blushes Scarlet deep,
> As if it fear'd the stroke which I intend,
> Like that of Jupiter — Lightning and Thunder:
> The Lords above are angry, and talk big,
> Or rather walk the mighty Cirque like Mourners
> Clad in long Clouds the robes of thickest Night,
> And seem to groan for Alexander's fall;
> 'Tis as Cassander's Soul cou'd wish it were,
> Which whensoe're it flies at lofty mischief
> Wou'd startle Fate and make all Heav'n concern'd.
> A mad Chaldean in the dead of Night
> Came to my Bed-side with a flaming Torch;
> And bellowing o're me like a Spirit damn'd,
> It cry'd, Well had it been for Babylon,
> If curs'd Cassander never had been born.[1]

Other conspirators come in, Thessalus and his brother Philip,
and Polyperchon, and there is a detailed account of the tor-
turing of Philotas, an earlier opponent of Alexander. There are
reminiscences of Shakespeare's Cassius speaking of Caesar in
one speech by Cassander.

> Remember he's a Man, his Flesh as soft
> And penetrable as a Girls: we have seen him wounded,
> A Stone has struck him, yet no Thunderbolt:

[1] I, i, 133–50.

> A Pebble fell'd this Jupiter along,
> A Sword has cut him, a Javelin pierc'd him,
> Water will drown him, Fire burn him.
> A Surfeit, nay a Fit of Common-sickness,
> Brings this Immortal to the Gate of Death.[1]

The confusion of purpose is made worse because this scene has to introduce not only the conspiracy, but also the rivalry between the two Queens. Cassander enjoins secrecy.

> Remember Hermolaus, and be hush'd.
> *Polyperchon:* Still, as the Bosome of the desart Night,
> As fatal Planets, or deep plotting Fiends.

Cassander at this point most abruptly changes the subject.

> Today he comes to Babylon from Susa
> With proud Roxana.[2]

The only excuse for what happens now can be that Lee felt the scene was beginning to drag.

> Ha! who's that, — look here.
> Enter the Ghost of King Philip, shaking a Trunchion at 'em, walks over the Stage.

(We must beware again. Truncheons in those days did not signify police constables. They were the batons of military commanders.) The dreadful apparition, however, only disconcerts them for fourteen lines.[3] Then —

> Pray to the business.

Cassander continues,

> As I was saying,

(It is not the only time in the play that Lee uses this feeble conversational phrase when he wants to pick up the thread again.)

---

[1] I, i, 266–73.

[2] I, i, 281–5. (All the early texts have 'from Babylon to Susa', which is clearly wrong.)

[3] Early in the eighteenth century the appearance of Philip's ghost was dropped from performances of the play.

> As I was saying, this Roxana whom
> To aggravate my hate to him I love,
> Meeting him as he came Triumphant from
> The Indies, kept him Revelling at Susa;
> But as I found, a deep repentance since
> Turns his affections to the Queen Statira,
> To whom he swore, before he cou'd espouse her,
> That he wou'd never Bed Roxana more.[1]

The reference to Cassander's love for Roxana seems astonishingly casual, but I suppose it is no more so than Iago's reference to the fact that he believes Emilia had been unfaithful to him with Othello.

Cassander tells how he had done his best to fan Statira's jealousy of Roxana and the conspirators depart.

> Enter Sysigambis, Statira, Parisatis, Attendants.

The following scene is of great importance. For the first time one of the main protagonists appears. Statira has to establish not only her own character, but also her love for Alexander. It is of the essence of the dramatic conflict in the play, which will in due course lead to two scenes of passionate encounter, that Statira and Roxana should be different and that their love for Alexander should be different also. Lee, I think, manages this with great success. Statira is shown to be gentle, faithful, affectionate, still deeply in love with Alexander and her love for him is almost maternal.

> *Statira:*   Away, and let me dye,
>   O 'tis my fondness, and my easie Nature
>   That wou'd excuse him; but I know he's false,
>   'Tis now the common talk, the news o' th' World,
>   False to Statira, false to her that lov'd him,
>   That lov'd him, cruel Victor as he was,
>   And took him bath'd all o're with Persian Blood;
>   Kiss'd the dear cruel Wounds, and wash'd 'em o're
>   And o're in Tears, — then bound 'em with my Hair,
>   Laid him all Night upon my panting Bosome,
>   Lull'd like a Child, and hush'd him with my Songs.

[1] I, i, 300–8.

Parisatis: If this be true, ah, who will ever trust
    A Man again?
Statira: A Man! a Man! my Parisatis
    Thus with my hand held up, thus let me swear thee.
    By the eternal Body of the Sun,
    Whose Body, O forgive the Blasphemy,
    I lov'd not half so well as the least part
    Of my dear precious faithless Alexander;
    For I will tell thee, and to warn thee of him,
    Not the Springs Mouth, nor Breath of Jesamin,
    Nor Violets Infant sweets, nor opening Buds
    Are half so sweet as Alexander's Breast,
    From every Pore of him a perfume falls,
    He kisses softer than a Southern Wind;
    Curls like a Vine, and touches like a God.
Sysigambis: When will thy Spirits rest, these transports cease?
Statira: Will you not give me leave to warn my Sister?
    As I was saying — but I told his sweetness,
    Then he will talk, good Gods how he will talk!
    Even when the joy he sigh'd for is possest,
    He speaks the kindest words and looks such things,
    Vows with such Passion, swears with so much grace,
    That 'tis a kind of Heaven to be deluded by him.[1]

But the scene has a further purpose. Statira vows that she
will never meet Alexander again. This vow has to brood over
the rest of the play. It must never be forgotten. Lee, I think,
accomplishes his purpose.

Statira: Madam, draw near, with all that are in presence,
    And list'n to the Vow which here I make.
Sysigambis: Take heed my dear Statira, and consider
    What desperate Love enforces you to swear.
Statira: Pardon me, for I have considered well;
    And here I bid adieu to all Mankind.
    Farewel ye Cozners of the easie Sex,
    And thou the greatest, falsest Alexander;
    Farewel though most belov'd, thou faithless Dear;

[1] I, i, 351–83.

If I but mention him, the Tears will fall;
Sure there is not a Letter in his Name
But is a Charm, to melt a Womans Eyes.
Sysigambis: Clear up thy griefs, thy King, thy Alexander
Comes on to Babylon.
Statira: Why let him come,
Joy of all Eyes, but the forlorn Statira's.
Sysigambis: Wilt thou not see him?
Statira: By Heav'n, I never will.
This is my Vow, my sacred Resolution; (She kneels)
And when I break it —
Sysigambis: Ah, do not ruine all.
Statira: May I again be flatter'd and deluded,
May sudden death and horrid, come instead
Of what I wish, and take me unprepar'd.
Sysigambis: Still kneel, and with the same Breath call agen
The woful Imprecation thou hast made.
Statira: No, I will publish it through all the Court,
Then in the Bowers of great Semiramis
For ever lock my woes from human view.
Sysigambis: Yet be perswaded.
Statira: Never urge me more.[1]

Sysigambis's terrified anxiety at the vow should prepare us for what will happen.

It will be noted that Alexander has not yet appeared. He is being built up as an heroic figure. A delayed appearance of this kind is used in the same way in other heroic plays, such as Addison's *Cato*. Dryden had advocated it in his *Essay on Dramatic Poesy*, citing Ben Jonson, who so managed things that 'before [his characters] come upon the stage, you have a longing expectation of them, which prepares you to receive them favourably; and when they are there, even from the first appearance you are so far acquainted with them, that nothing of their humour is lost to you'.[2]

The Second Act begins with a very elaborate piece of machinery.

[1] I, i, 404–30.   [2] *Essays of John Dryden*, I, 87–8.

Noise of Trumpets sounding far off. The Scene draws, and discovers a Battel of Crows, or Ravens, in the Air; an Eagle and a Dragon meet and fight; the Eagle drops down with all the rest of the Birds, and the Dragon flies away. Souldiers walk off, shaking their heads. The Conspirators come forward.

> *Cassander:* He comes, the fatal glory of the World,
> The headlong Alexander, with a Guard
> Of thronging Crowns comes on to Babylon,
> Tho' warn'd, in spight of all the Powr's above,
> Who by these Prodigies foretell his ruine.[1]

The plotters tell of the coming also of Roxana, 'jealous, bloody and ambitious', burning for revenge against Statira, whom they hope to win over to their side. (We may note that whenever Cassander is on the stage there are continually reminiscences of Shakespeare in the verse.) Lysimachus and Hephestion come in, and then Clytus and Aristander, a soothsayer. The trumpets sound nearer; others crowd on to the stage, the Chaldean priests, Nearchus and Eumenes; and then —

Enter Alexander, all kneel but Clytus.

(At this point from the 1780's it was customary for a chorus of soldiers to sing 'See, the conquering hero comes', a song written for Handel's oratorio *Joshua*, and subsequently transferred to his *Judas Maccabeus*.) Alexander greets his captains severally and opens unexpectedly quietly; it is only when he speaks with Clytus about the Battle of the Granicus that he becomes rhetorical. This speech was quoted by Colley Cibber as an example of Lee at his most absurd.[2] I should not go so far as Bishop Warburton, who said that it contained not only the most sublime, but the most judicious imagery that poetry can conceive. But I think Lee knew what he was about. He was from the start emphasising this incident, which is frequently referred to in the play, because it serves to link

[1] II, i, 1–5.

[2] *An Apology for the Life of Mr Colley Cibber*, ed. R. W. Lowe (1889), I, 105–6.

Alexander with Clytus, who saved his life there, and to remind one of the hero Alexander once had been.

Aristander, who was obviously intended to play the same part as the soothsayer in *Julius Caesar*, warns him to leave Babylon, and Perdiccas and Meleager enter to tell a dreadful story of ravens they have just seen fighting a great battle in the sky. Lysimachus claims the hand of Parisatis, which had been promised to Hephestion, and is told never to ask for it again. Sysigambis and Parisatis come in and Alexander is told of Statira's jealousy of Roxana and of her vow never to see him again.

> *Alexander:* Ha! did she swear? did that sweet Creature
> swear?
> I'le not believe it, no, she is all softness,
> All melting, mild, and calm as a rock'd Infant,
> Nor can you wake her into cryes: by Heaven,
> She is the Child of Love, and she was born in smiles.[1]

Alexander implores the two women to persuade Statira to relent. Lysimachus rashly presses his suit once more and Alexander, exasperated, orders Perdiccas to take him and throw him to a lion. (Lee, in working out the absurd theme of the love of Lysimachus for Parisatis, was following la Calprenède's novel.) The whole act is not very inspired — some of it, indeed, is very flat — and what action there is is provided by the introductory stage machinery, but at least Alexander is not yet the 'mad hero, drawn by a mad poet', as described by Steele.

The Third Act opens with Lysimachus being led away by Perdiccas under guard and they meet Parisatis. The scene is quite a perfunctory one. And then Philip, one of the conspirators says,

> See where the jealous proud Roxana comes,
> A haughty vengeance gathers up her brow,[2]

and Roxana enters with Cassander and Polyperchon.

There is no denying that Roxana rants, but Lee has to draw quickly a picture of a woman who is the very opposite of

[1] II, i, 350–4.   [2] III, i, 34–5.

Statira, one passionately vehement in her love and jealousy, an Amazonian figure. She is told that Alexander is endeavouring to persuade Statira to accept him once more.

> *Roxana:* Away, be gone, and give a whirlwind room,
> Or I will blow you up like dust; avaunt:
> Madness but meanly represents my toyl.

(These are the lines which Steele attributed to Alexander.)

> Roxana, and Statira, they are names
> That must for ever jarr: eternal discord,
> Fury, revenge, disdain, and indignation
> Tear my swoln breast, make way for fire and tempest.
> My brain is burst, debate and reason quench'd,
> The storm is up, and my hot bleeding heart
> Splits with the rack, while passions like the winds
> Rise up to Heav'n, and put out all the Stars.[1]

She tells them of herself as a girl before she had heard of Alexander.

> When in my nonage I at Zogdia liv'd,
> Amongst my She-companions I would reign;
> Drew 'em from idleness, and little arts
> Of coining looks, and laying snares for Lovers,
> Broke all their Glasses, and their Tires tore,
> Taught 'em, like Amazons, to ride and chace
> Wild beasts in Desarts, and to Master men.[2]

She speaks of Alexander as a lover,

> Gods! that a man should be so great and base!
> What said he not when in the Bridal Bed,
> He clasp'd my yielding body in his arms . . .
> He swore the Globe of Heav'n and Earth were vile
> To those rich Worlds: and talk'd, and kiss'd, and lov'd,
> And made me shame the morning with my blushes.[3]

(Obviously the audience is meant to recall Statira's very different words on Alexander talking.)

Statira enters with Sysigambis. She is on her way to fulfil

[1] III, i, 45–55.   [2] III, i, 77–83.   [3] III, i, 106–13.

her vow and, while Sysigambis makes a last attempt to persuade her to renounce it, which she resists, Roxana stands in the background and comments.

> She shews a certain bravery of Soul,
> Which I shou'd praise in any but my Rival.[1]

Then Roxana steps forward and for the first time the Rival Queens meet face to face.

The scene that follows is a very effective one. There is no doubt that the popularity of the play depended — apart from the character of Alexander, which so many great actors felt to be a rewarding part (their opportunities were to come later in the play) — on the two great scenes where the rivals meet. Roxana is at first touched by Statira's resignation.

> I hope your Majesty will give me leave
> To wait you to the Grove, where you wou'd grieve:
> Where like the Turtle, you the loss will moan
> Of that dear Mate, and murmur all alone.[2]

But this merely serves to rouse Statira.

> How frail, how cowardly is woman's mind ?
> We shriek at Thunder, dread the rustling wind,
> And glitt'ring Swords the brightest eyes will blind.
> Yet when strong Jealousie enflames the Soul,
> The weak will roar, and Calms to Tempests roul.
> Rival, take heed, and tempt me not too far;
> My bloud may boyl, and blushes shew a War.[3]

Now Roxana is roused too and begins to taunt her rival.

> When you retire to your Romantick Cell,
> I'le make thy solitary mansion Hell;
> Thou shalt not rest by day, nor sleep by night,
> But still Roxana shall thy Spirit fright:
> Wanton, in Dreams, if thou dars't dream of bliss,
> Thy roving Ghost may think to steal a kiss;
> But when to his sought Bed, thy wandring air
> Shall for the happiness it wish'd repair,

[1] III, i, 165–6.   [2] III, i, 195–8.   [3] III, i, 218–24.

How will it groan to find thy Rival there?
How ghastly wilt thou look, when thou shalt see,
Through the drawn Curtains, that Great man and me,
Wearied with laughing joys.[1]

(Lee, it may be noted, is writing in rhyme. Like Dryden, he
had only recently discarded the rhymed couplet.)

And now Roxana succeeds where Sysigambis and all the rest
have failed.

> *Statira:* 'Tis well, I thank thee; thou hast wak'd a rage,
>   Whose boiling now no temper can asswage:
>   I meet thy tides of Jealousie with more,
>   Dare thee to duel, and dash thee o're and o're.
> *Roxana:* What wou'd you dare?
> *Statira:*   Whatever you dare do,
>   My warring thoughts the bloudiest tracts pursue,
>   I am by Love a Fury made, like you:
>   Kill, or be kill'd, thus acted by despair.
> *Roxana:* Sure the disdain'd Statira does not dare.
> *Statira:* Yes, tow'ring proud Roxana, but I dare.
> *Roxana:* I tow'r indeed o're thee:
>   Like a fair Wood, the shade of Kings I stand,
>   While thou, sick Weed, dost but infect the Land.
> *Statira:* No, like an Ivy I will curl thee round,
>   Thy sapless Trunk of all its pride confound,
>   Then dry, and wither'd, bend thee to the ground.
>   What Sysigambis threats, objected fears,
>   My Sisters sighs, and Alexander's tears,
>   Cou'd not effect, thy Rival rage has done;
>   My Soul, whose start at breach of oaths begun,
>   Shall to thy ruine violated run.
>   I'le see the King, in spight of all I swore,
>   Though curst that thou mayst never see him more.[2]

Alexander now returns and implores Statira to forgive him.
Roxana throws herself between them, but she is rejected and
she storms out, swearing vengeance.

[1] III, i, 225–86.
[2] III, i, 248–70. (Quarto 4, in line 251, corrects dwell to duel.)

Statira, however, though she breaks her oath in speaking to Alexander, will go no further. As Roxana departs, she says,

> O Alexander, is it possible? Good Gods,
> That guilt can shew so lovely! yet I pardon,
> Forgive thee all, by thy dear life I do.
> *Alexander:* Ha, Pardon! said'st thou, Pardon me? . . .
> Is it then true that thou hast pardon'd me?
> And is it giv'n me thus to touch thy hand,
> And fold thy body in my longing arms?
> To gaze upon thy Eyes, my happier Stars?
> To tast thy lip, and thy dear balmy breath,
> While ev'ry sigh comes forth so fraught with sweets,
> 'Tis incense to be offer'd to a God.
> *Statira:* Yes, dear Impostor, 'tis most true that I
> Have pardon'd thee, and tis as true that while
> I stand in view of thee, thy eyes will wound,
> Thy tongue will make me wanton as thy wishes;
> And while I feel thy hand, my body glows:
> Therefore be quick; and take your last adieu,
> These your last sighs, and these your parting tears;
> Farewell, farewell, a long and last farewell.
> *Alexander:* O my Hephestion, bear me or I sink.
> *Statira:* Nay, you may take — Heav'n how my heart throbs,
> You may, you may, if yet you think me worthy,
> Take from these trembling lips a parting kiss.
> *Alexander:* No, let me starve first — why, Statira, why?
> What is the meaning of all this? O gods![1]

He wrestles desperately to make her relent and in one speech at least he speaks in the language for which Lee was first admired and later scorned.

> Yes, I will shake this Cupid from my arms,
> If all the rages of the Earth can fright him;
> Drown him in the deep bowl of Hercules;
> Make the World drunk, and then, like Aeolus,
> When he gave passage to the struggling winds,
> I'le strike my Spear into the reeling Globe

[1] III, i, 318–44.

E

> To let it bloud; set Babylon in a blaze
> And drive this God of flames with more consuming fire.[1]

But there was method in Lee's madness. It was not Alexander's rant which was to win his battle, but his retreat from ranting. He admits defeat.

> O my Statira!
> I swear, my Queen, I'le not out-live thy hate.
> My Soul is still as death. — But one thing more,
> Pardon my last extremities,

(that is his 'ranting')

> the transports
> Of a deep wounded breast, and all is well.
> *Statira:* Rise, and may Heav'n forgive you all, like me.
> *Alexander:* You are too gracious. Clytus, bear me hence.
> When I am laid in Earth, yield her the world.
> There's something here heaves, and is cold as Ice,
> That stops my breath. — Farewell, O Gods! for ever.

And then Statira throws her oath to the winds.

> Hold off, and let me run into his arms,
> My dearest, my all Love, my Lord, my King.
> You shall not dye, if that the soul and body
> Of thy Statira can restore thy life:
> Give me thy wonted kindness, bend me, break me
> With thy embraces.[2]

The scene ends in an ecstasy of rejoicing and Alexander invites all his captains to a banquet, a banquet at which he is to meet his end. We know — or we should do — that Statira is doomed.

I think we can understand how this act, from the first appearance of Roxana to its unexpected end, came to hold the stage. It is rhetorical, sometimes violently so, but Lee never lets his rhetoric get completely out of control. 'There is an infinite fire in his works,' Addison said, 'but so involved in smoke that it does not appear in half its lustre.'[3] The charge is often justified, but not in this scene. Lee's management of the

---

[1] III, i, 376–83.   [2] III, i, 400–14.   [3] *The Spectator*, No. 39.

changes in fortune and of the passionate encounters seems to
me masterly. And, it may be noted, there is no violent action
at all; in fact, the only action throughout is when, towards the
end of the act, Alexander calls on all his captains to kneel with
him as he beseeches Statira to relent.

There is action enough in the next act, however. It is divided
into two scenes. It begins, 'Enter Clytus in his Macedonian
habit; Hephestion, Eumenes, Meleager, &c. in Persian robes.'
Later we shall see enacted the death of Clytus, which is an
historical incident, though it actually occurred much earlier.
Lee took this largely from Quintus Curtius. Clytus has had no
part in the last act except at the very end when he begs to be
excused the banquet, but Alexander insists on his attendance.
He is now to act as a reminder of Alexander's earlier days,
before he had succumbed to the corruption of power and love.

> I'le go, my Friends, in this old Habit thus,
> And laugh, and drink the King's health heartily;
> And while you blushing bow your heads to earth,
> And hide 'em in the dust, I'll stand upright,
> Strait as a Spear, the Pillar of my country,
> And be by so much nearer to the Gods.[1]

Alexander comes in with Statira and her sister. Parisatis
pleads for Lysimachus's life and, when Statira adds her en-
treaties, Alexander relents and sends some of his captains to
prevent Perdiccas throwing him to the lion. Statira then says
that she will go to the bower of Semiramis to await Alexander.
They move to go on to the banquet when Roxana appears with
the conspirators and declares that Alexander will never enjoy
the love of Statira. Alexander passes her unconcerned and
Roxana is left with the conspirators. Lee clearly felt that it was
necessary to do something to restore her position in the eyes
of the audience before the final meeting of the Rival Queens.
Cassander now woos her and is scornfully rejected. This is not a
successful scene and Roxana's rhetoric becomes at times very
bombastic.

[1] IV, i, 35–40.

> No, if I were a wanton, I wou'd make
> Princes the Victims of my raging fires:
> I, like the changing Moon, wou'd have the Stars
> My followers, and mantled Kings by night
> Shou'd wait my call.[1]

To Cassander's suggestion, however, that she should murder
Statira immediately, during the banquet, she agrees ecstatic-
ally. Cassander makes the final arrangements for the murder
of Alexander; a poison is to be dropped into his wine, which
will kill him in five hours. We hear nothing more of this, and
the conspiracy seems to be entirely forgotten in the banquet-
scene that follows. It is not until towards the end of the next
act that one is suddenly reminded of it when Alexander exclaims,

> What means this deadly dew upon my forehead?

Rarely can a murder have been more casually depicted on the
stage. Lee showed in other plays that he could manage a
murder by poisoning as well as any other. But from first to last,
this sub-plot in *The Rival Queens* is bungled. The conspirators
now leave, some to the banquet, others with Roxana to the
bower of Semiramis, and —

> The Scene draws, Alexander is seen standing on a Throne
> with all his Commanders about him, holding Goblets in their
> hands.

But unfortunately Lee had first to take up the theme of
Lysimachus. The captains, who had been sent with the reprieve,
come in 'leading in Lysimachus in his shirt bloudy'. It is really
impossible to tell how Lee meant this scene to be acted.
Alexander seems to think that Lysimachus is dead, although
he is on the stage, and Hephestion says, 'Your mercy flew too
late.' But Clytus then describes how Lysimachus, when faced
with the lion slew it. His language deserves all that the critics
were to say of Lee.

> And, as the Lyon turn'd,
> Thrust Gauntlet, arm and all, into his throat,

[1] IV, i, 198–202.

And with Herculean force tore forth by th' roots
The foaming bloudy tongue; and while the Savage,
Faint with that loss, sunk to the blushing Earth
To plough it with his teeth, your conqu'ring Souldier
Leap'd on his back, and dash'd his skull to pieces.[1]

It is no excuse that the whole is taken straight from la Calprenède. Quintus Curtius, however, was a better model. The death of Clytus which follows is superbly managed and must have been extremely effective on the stage.

The quarrel begins when Lysimachus offers Clytus a Persian robe, which he refuses.

Clytus: O vanity!
Alexander: Ha! What says Clytus? Who am I?
Clytus: The Son of good King Philip.
Alexander: No, 'tis false;
  By all my Kindred in the Skies,
  Jove made my Mother pregnant.
Clytus: I ha' done.[2]

Then, as there follows 'an entertainment of Indian singers and dancers' and 'the Musick flourishes', Alexander and Clytus drink deep.

Alexander: Now let us talk
  Of War, for what more fits a Souldiers mouth?
  And speak, speak freely, or ye do not love me,
  Who think you was the bravest General
  That ever led an Army to the Field?
Hephestion: I think the Sun himself ne're saw a Chief
  So truly great, so fortunately brave,
  As Alexander; not the fam'd Alcides,
  Nor fierce Achilles. . . .
Lysimachus: Such was not Cyrus.
Alexander: O you flatter me.
Clytus: They do indeed, and yet you love 'em for it,
  But hate old Clytus, for his hardy Virtue.
  Come, shall I speak a man more brave than you,
  A better General, and more expert Souldier?

[1] IV, i, 317–23.   [2] IV, i, 354–8.

Alexander: I shou'd be glad to learn, instruct me, Sir.

Clytus: Your Father Philip. — I have seen him March
  And fought beneath his dreadful Banner, where
  The stoutest at this Table would ha' trembled:
  Nay frown not, Sir, you cannot look me dead.
  When Greeks joyn'd Greeks, then was the tug of War,
  The labour'd Battle sweat, and Conquest bled.
  Why should I fear to speak a truth more noble
  Than e're your Father Jupiter Ammon told you;
  Philip fought men, but Alexander women![1]

In a drunken fury Alexander boasts of his military prowess and
then throws fruit at Clytus. (This strange incident comes
straight from Plutarch.) Clytus sneeringly reminds him how he
had saved his life at the battle of the Granicus. Alexander
makes a last effort to control himself.

  Go, leave the Banquet; thus far I forgive thee.

But Clytus will not spare him now.

  Forgive yourself for all your Blasphemies,
  The riots of a most debauch'd, and blotted life,
  Philotas murder — [2]

At this, Alexander, now quite beside himself, seizes a javelin
from one of the guards. The rest strive to part them, but
Alexander strikes him through and Clytus falls dead before
him. At once he is overwhelmed with remorse.

  Then I am lost, what has my vengeance done?
  Who is it thou hast slain? Clytus: what was he?
  The faithful Subject, worthiest Counsellor,
  Who for saving of thy life, when
  Thou foughtst Bare-headed at the River Granike,
  Has now a noble Recompense; for speaking rashly;
  For a forgetfulness which wine did work,
  The poor, the honest Clytus thou hast slain![3]

[1] IV, i, 401–25.   [2] IV, i, 471–4.
[3] IV, i, 510–16. (I give here the text of the Second and subsequent
Quartos.

Inconsolable, he falls by Clytus's side. But suddenly there are 'Cries without, Arm, arm, Treason, Treason! Enter Perdiccas, bloudy'. He calls out that

> Roxana, fill'd with furious Jealousie,
> Came with a Guard of Zogdean Slaves unmark'd,

and had entered the Bower of Semiramis. Alexander rises,

> Thus from the Grave I rise to save my Love,
> All draw your Swords, with wings of Lightning move;
> When I rush on, sure none will dare to stay,
> 'Tis Beauty calls, and Glory shews the way.[1]

'Statira', the last Act opens, 'is discover'd sleeping in the Bower of Semiramis.' The spirits of her father, Darius, and her mother stand over her and sing a song, warning her of disaster. Statira awakes; at first she is frightened, but she puts the dream from her thoughts and eagerly awaits Alexander. She thinks she hears him coming, but 'Enter Roxana, with Slaves and a dagger'.

The final scene between the Rival Queens was very famous and many a great actress wished to play her part in it. It is not long, only eighty lines. It is not, as one might have expected, a mere shouting-match. It is in fact very exciting. The audience knows that Alexander is hastening to save Statira. She plays for time and begins by trying to cow Roxana.

> And what is she, who with such Tow'ring pride
> Wou'd awe a Princess that is born above her?
> *Roxana:* I like the Port Imperial Beauty bears,
> It shews thou hast a Spirit fit to fall
> A sacrifice to fierce Roxana's wrongs. . . .[2]

Statira, apparently unmoved, attempts to pass her,

> Yet I disdain to stand the Fate you offer,
> And therefore fearless of thy dreadful threats,
> Walk thus regardless by thee.
> *Roxana:*   Ha! so stately!
> This sure will sink you.

(No doubt at this point she shows her dagger.)

[1] IV, i, 564–5, 574–7.   [2] V, i, 53–7.

    Statira: No, Roxana, no;
       The blow you give will strike me to the Stars,
       But sink my murdress in Eternal ruine.[1]

Roxana, for a moment, weakens.

    Roxana: Heav'n witness for me, I would spare thy life,
       If anything but Alexander's Love
       Were in debate; come give me back his heart,
       And thou shalt live, live Empress of the world.
    Statira: The world is less than Alexander's Love,
       Yet cou'd I give it, 'tis not in my power:
       This I dare promise, if you spare my life,
       Which I disdain to beg, he shall speak kindly.
    Roxana: Speak! is that all?
    Statira: Perhaps at my request,
       And for a gift so noble as my life,
       Bestow a kiss.
    Roxana: A kiss! no more?
    Statira: O Gods!
       What shall I say to work her to my end?
       Fain would I see him — yes, a little more,
       Embrace you, and for ever be your Friend.

With those words Statira seals her fate.

    Roxana: O, the provoking word! Your Friend! Thou dy'st:
       Your Friend![2]

Statira makes one last attempt.

    But O, Roxana, that there may appear
    A glimpse of Justice for thy Cruelty,
    A grain of Goodness, for a mass of Evil,
    Give me my Death in Alexander's presence.
    Roxana: Not for the Rule of Heav'n: — are you so cunning?
       What you wou'd have him mourn you as you fall?
       Take your farewell, and taste such healing kisses,
       As might call back your Soul?[3]

A Slave bursts in and announces that Alexander is at the gates.

   [1] V, i, 65–70.   [2] V, i, 81–96.   [3] V, i, 105–12.

Roxana: Then I must haste. (She stabs her.)
Statira: What is the King so near?
And shall I dye so tamely, thus defenceless?
O ye good Gods! will you not help my weakness?
Roxana: They are far off. (She stabs her again.)
Statira: Alas! They are indeed.[1]

Alexander rushes in, but it is too late, and Statira dies in his arms.

The scene is melodrama and there is no doubt that it was played as such. The story is told of two famous actresses playing the parts, who were rivals in more senses than one. Mrs Barry, as Roxana, was furious because the tiring-master had allotted to Mrs Bowteel, as Statira, the veil she wanted, and she stabbed her so fiercely that the knife penetrated her stays and half an inch into her flesh. It is also said that Mrs Woffington, as Roxana, once threatened Mrs Bellamy so violently that she retreated from the stage, and then, in the presence of Alexander and his soldiers waiting for their cue and nearly in view of the audience, Mrs Woffington stabbed her in good earnest. Whether we think the scene is more than melodrama will depend largely on our judgment of the whole play. At any rate, it must be allowed to be good melodrama.

Lee must have been puzzled what to do with Roxana. According to all the canons of heroic tragedy she ought to have died. We are told in the most casual way that Sysigambis has died on hearing of Statira's death and that 'your dear Hephestion, having drunk too largely at your last feast, is of a surfeit dead'. But even Lee could hardly so tamper with history as to kill off Roxana, who was to give birth to Alexander's heir after his death. So Statira, pathetic to the last and here, perhaps, absurdly so, pleads in her dying words that she may be spared. Roxana's final scene with Alexander, after Statira's death, is indeed fustian, but Lee has one twist at the end which is unexpected. Roxana's love for Alexander turns at the last to hatred and she leaves the stage cursing him.

[1] V, i, 119–23.

There remains the death of Alexander. Here, indeed, we
have 'the mad hero', but he has been poisoned and is in the
frenzy of delirium. It is not mere ranting. Lee has a definite
purpose in this last scene; he must restore Alexander as a hero.
There are some remarkably skilful touches. Parmenio, Philotas
and Clytus, the men whom he had murdered because they would
not accept him as a god, are his companions once more. Like
another great military leader on his deathbed, he is '*tête
d'armée*'. We should not take too much amiss elements in this
scene which were merely part of the conventional treatment of
delirium or madness, such as Alexander's laughter.

> *Alexander:* Ha, ha, ha, I shall dye with laughter.
> Parmenio, Clytus, dost thou see yon fellow ?
> That ragged Souldier, that poor tatter'd Greek ?
> See how he puts to flight the gaudy Persians,
> With nothing but a rusty Helmet on, through which
> The grizly bristles of his pushing Beard
> Drive 'em like Pikes.[1]

'The poor tatter'd Greek', now at the last seen at his true
worth against 'the gaudy Persians', with all Alexander's
Captains standing round him in Persian robes, is enough, I
think, to show how skilfully Lee is managing this final scene.

> Sound, sound, keep your Ranks close, ay now they come:
> O the brave din, the noble clank of Arms!
> Charge, Charge apace, and let the Phalanx move.
> Darius comes — ha! let me in, none dare
> To cross my fury; — Philotas is unhors'd; — Ay, 'tis
> Darius,
> I see, I know him by his sparkling Plumes,
> And his Gold Chariot drawn by ten white Horses:
> But like a Tempest thus I pour upon him, —
> He bleeds, with that last blow I brought him down;
> They fly, they fly, — follow, follow, — Victoria, Victoria,
> Victoria.[2]

But the hero must not die in a frenzy. Alexander's last words
(Lee is at first following Curtius) are certainly moving.

[1] V, i, 334-40.   [2] V, i, 342-53.

Let me embrace you all before I dye:
Weep not, my dear Companions, the good Gods
Shall send you in my stead a nobler Prince,
One that shall lead you forth with matchless conduct.
Lysimachus: Break not our hearts with such unkind
                                        expressions.
Perdiccas: We will not part with you, nor change for Mars.
Alexander: Perdiccas, take this Ring.
   And see me laid in the Temple of
   Jupiter Ammon.
Lysimachus: To whom does your dread Majesty bequeath
   The Empire of the World?
Alexander: To him that is most worthy.
Perdiccas: When will you, sacred sir, that we should give
   To your great memory those Divine Honours,
   Which such exalted Virtue does deserve?
Alexander: When you are all most happy, and in peace.
   Your hands. —

(The last lines are Lee's own; they are not to be found in any
of his sources.)

               O Father, if I have discharg'd
      The duty of a man to Empire born:
      If by unwearied toil I have deserv'd
      The vast renown of thy adopted Son,
      Accept this Soul, which thou didst first inspire,
      And with this sigh, thus gives thee back again.[1]

Well, there it is. It is a play full of faults. Never could sub-
plots have been less convincingly managed. The fire, to use
Addison's expression, is often involved in smoke. But it should
not surprise us that it held the stage so long. Lee had one gift,
at least, in full measure. He understood the theatre. And
whatever our judgment may be, it is not a minor work. It is
grandly planned. I am glad to have been able to speak of this
play of its most unhappy author, as a guest of the College of
which, in his happier days, he had been a member.

                    [1] V, i, 360–81.

III

Edward Young
Night Thoughts

EDWARD Young has a most unusual position in English literary history. Except by those who have a professional interest, as teachers or students, his poetry is never read. In that sense he is as lost as the other two writers of whom I have spoken, William Warner and Nathaniel Lee. But his name and that of his greatest work are not only remembered; they are household words. No doubt William Blake's illustrations to the *Night Thoughts* play their part now in preventing the names being forgotten. But those who admire these illustrations do not read the poem. I must try to show why this poem made so deep an impression on his own age and on the generation which followed his, enough for Boswell to regard it as 'a mass of the grandest and richest poetry that human genius has ever produced',[1] for Johann Andreas Cremer, founder of the Bremer Beiträger, one of the first groups in the literary awakening of Germany, to consider it superior to Milton and only just below the Psalms, the Prophets and the Book of Revelation,[2] for Robespierre in his days of power to have carried a copy about with him in his pocket,[3] for Coleridge to have made a habit of reading a passage or two and of then going off for a solitary walk, simply to ruminate on the ideas it gave

[1] *Boswell's Life of Johnson*, ed. G. B. Hill and L. F. Powell, (Oxford, 1934), IV, 60.

[2] L. M. Price, *English Literature in Germany* (University of California, 1953), 114.

[3] W. Thomas, *Le Poète Edward Young* (Paris, 1901), 539.

him.[1] There must be something remarkable about a poem which could do all that and yet, two hundred years after it was written, can do nothing at all. But we shall not understand the poem and the impression which it made if we think of it as material for illustration by a great artist. The first service we can do Edward Young is to forget, for the moment, William Blake.

Young was born in 1683 and died in 1765. The length of his life is significant. For he was not one of those poets who live on, a respected figure of a past literary age, into one which thinks and writes quite differently; nor was he one whose later work seems to be the culmination of his writings as a young man, in the way that, for instance, Milton's *Paradise Lost* is organically linked with his *Nativity Ode*. Young was a minor poet and was not thought of as anything else until the first four books of his *Night Thoughts* were published, and this was in 1742, when he was fifty-nine years old. His most original work, *Conjectures on Original Composition*, was written when he was seventy-six. There were some connections between his earlier and later works. In 1713 Addison's *Cato* was published with eight com mendatory poems. The third was by Edward Young, who was then almost unknown. One of the chief reasons why, nearly fifty years later, he wrote the *Conjectures on Original Composition*, which was a revolutionary piece of criticism, was to extol the works of Addison and to tell the affecting — to us the quite uncomfortably affecting — story of Addison's deathbed, how in his dying words he had exclaimed, 'See, in what peace a Christian can die!' One of Young's earliest poems, *The Last Day*, stands out among the rest in foreshadowing the style and feeling of the *Night Thoughts*. But one cannot possibly say that his poems as a young man seem to lead naturally to the works he wrote later in life.

Edward Young's father, who had the same Christian name, had been educated at Winchester and New College and in 1678 became Chaplain to the Earl of Ossory, who commanded the

[1] *The Table Talk and Omniana of Samuel Taylor Coleridge* (Oxford, 1917), p. 315.

English forces in Flanders. He returned next year and the
Earl recommended him to his father, the great Duke of
Ormonde, with the charming tribute, 'He is eminent both for
preaching and good living, and not being troublesome. Besides,
he is an Oxford man.'[1] Ormonde, however, was unwilling or
unable to help, and Young became a Fellow of Winchester and
Rector of Upham, a New College living. There the poet,
Edward Young, was born. He went to Winchester in 1695 and,
failing to secure a scholarship, to New College as a commoner
in 1702. Next year he transferred to Corpus Christi College and
in 1708, at the age of twenty-five, he became a Law Fellow of
All Souls College.

> Wickham! Fox! Chichley! hail, illustrious names,
> Who to far distant times dispense your beams;
> Beneath your shades, and near your crystal springs,
> I first presum'd to touch the trembling strings.[2]

Edward Young began to write poetry.

Nothing is more difficult than to assess the value of the
gossip of later days about the obscure early life of an author
who eventually becomes famous. Sir Herbert Croft, who wrote
the Life of Young, published as one of Johnson's *Lives of the
English Poets*, said that, 'When first Young found himself
independent and his own master at All Souls, he was not the
ornament to religion and morality which he afterwards
became.'[3] But Croft himself said that Tindal (of whom Dr
Johnson was wont to say, 'Don't forget that rascal Tindal, Sir.
Be sure to hang up the atheist,'[4]) used to meet Young at All
Souls and reported, 'The other boys I can always answer, because I always know whence they have their arguments, which
I have read a hundred times; but that fellow Young is continu-

[1] Henry C. Shelley, *The Life and Letters of Edward Young* (1914), 5.
[2] *The Last Day*, Book II.
[3] Samuel Johnson, *Lives of the English Poets*, ed. G. B. Hill (1905),
III, 364.
[4] Samuel Johnson, *Lives of the English Poets*, ed. P. Cunningham
(1854), III, 311, n. 6.

ally pestering me with something of his own.'[1] At any rate the orthodoxy of Young's verses was from the start impeccable. Another story told of him in his Oxford days was that 'when composing he would shut up his windows and sit by a lamp even at mid-day, nay that skulls, bones and instruments of death were among the ornaments of his study'.[2] We may reasonably regard this as *ben trovato*, but there is no doubt that his first considerable poem, *The Last Day*, published in 1713, was a macabre piece of work.

The theme was entirely conventional. Poets, good and bad, were at that time constantly writing on the terrors of Hell and on the final judgement of souls. What can be said is that Young dealt with his theme with unusual thoroughness. It had always been a scene hard to picture very exactly. Young shirked no difficulty. There are some fine lines in his poem, but also some of the most gloriously ridiculous in English literature, as when he tackled the problem of the literal resurrection of the body,

> Now charnels rattle; scatter'd limbs, and all
> The various bones, obsequious to the call,
> Self-mov'd, advance; the neck perhaps to meet
> The distant head; the distant legs the feet.
> Dreadful to view, see thro' the dusky sky
> Fragments of bodies in confusion fly.[3]

(Dryden, we might note, made a passing reference, and a very tactful and skilful one, to the same problem in his Ode to the Memory of Mrs Anne Killigrew.)

He was still a member of a small and undistinguished company of Oxford poets, but he now began to make the acquaintance of the larger literary world of London. Through his friend Tickell he came to know Addison; he is to be found on the fringes of the great quarrel between Addison and Pope; he visited Dublin and met Swift. (Long after he recalled going for

[1] *Lives of the English Poets*, ed. G. B. Hill, III, 364.

[2] Mitford, *Poetical Works of Edward Young*, xii. (The story was told by Glocester Ridley.)

[3] *The Last Day*, Book II.

'an evening's walk' with him and some others. Swift stopped and, when the others went on, Young returned. 'I found him fixed as a statue and earnestly gazing upward at a noble elm, which in its uppermost branches was much withered and decayed. Pointing at it, he said, "I shall be like that tree; I shall die at the top." ¹) He also met Voltaire and wrote three poetic plays, *Busiris, King of Egypt*, of which his biographer, Henry Shelley, declared, 'if a manager could be found with courage to make the test, it is highly probable that *Busiris* might capture even a twentieth century audience'² — the Life, I may say, was written in 1914; it seems to me even more improbable now — *The Revenge*, which became very popular, and *The Brothers*, not put on the stage until 1753, when it played 'to thin houses but eight nights'.³

So far all this has not been very impressive. But Young's next production was quite unexpected. Between 1725 and 1728 he published a series of seven satires, entitled *Love of Fame, the Universal Passion*. Joseph Warton's comment on them can hardly be bettered, 'A work that abounds in wit, observation on life, pleasantry, delicacy, urbanity, and the most well-bred raillery, without a single mark of spleen or ill-nature. These were the first characteristical satires in our language, and are written in an ease and facility of style very different from this author's other works.'⁴ Swift, it is true, thought that Young was not 'angry' enough. Two of the satires are not on the love of fame, but on women, a gallery of female types, such as the blue-stocking,

> O'er the *Belle-lettre* lovely Daphne reigns;
> Again the god Apollo wears her chains:
> With legs toss'd high, on her sophee she sits,
> Vouchsafing audience to contending wits:

---

¹ E. Young, *Conjectures on Original Composition*, ed. E. J. Morley (1918), 29.

² H. C. Shelley, *op. cit.*, 44.

³ *Correspondence of Samuel Richardson* (1804), VI, 246.

⁴ Joseph Warton, *An Essay on the Genius and Writings of Pope*, II (1782), 203.

Of each performance she's the final test;
One act read o'er, she prophesies the rest;
And then, pronouncing with decisive air,
Fully convinces all the town — *she's fair*.[1]

Johnson, surprisingly, called *The Universal Passion* 'a very great performance', but he qualified the praise with a criticism which seems justified, Young 'plays, indeed, only on the surface of life; he never penetrates the recesses of the mind'.[2]

With the publication of *The Universal Passion* Young, who was forty-five when the seventh satire was published, had become a poet to be reckoned with, but in 1728 he was ordained priest.[3] The usual explanation is that he had abandoned all hope of making a decent living out of writing; there is no evidence for this, but it is not at all unlikely. Throughout his life, whether seeking for remuneration in cash or preferment in the Church, Young had little luck with his patrons. He did not leave immediately the literary circles of London. He took Pope's side in the tremendous literary disturbance caused by *The Dunciad* and wrote *Two Epistles to Mr Pope* in 1730, which show at times an impressive control of the conventional satiric style. But the kind of elegant common-sense he shows in them, unadventurous but pleasantly competent, was very unlike the verse he was to write some ten years later.

In the same year as the appearance of the *Two Epistles* Young became Rector of Welwyn. There he was to remain for the rest of his life, thirty-five years, though no one could have worked harder to secure preferment. Soon after this he married a widow, Lady Elizabeth Lee, the daughter of the Earl of Lichfield. Their son, Frederick, was born in 1732, and three years later his wife's eldest daughter by her first marriage, Elizabeth, was married to Henry Temple, the eldest son of the

[1] *Op. cit.*, 'Satire V. On Women'.
[2] Samuel Johnson, *Lives of the English Poets*, III, 394.
[3] He had been ordained deacon in 1724. I owe this and certain other points where Shelley's biography must be corrected to the kindness of Mr H. B. Forster who is now engaged on a biography of Edward Young.

F

first Viscount Palmerston. Elizabeth Temple, however, became
consumptive. Young took her with him to winter in Nice, but
she died on the way at Lyons on 8 October 1736. Young lost
his wife in January 1740, and six months later Henry Temple,
to whom he was deeply attached, died also.[1] There can be no
doubt that it was these three deaths which led him to write the
opening books of the *Night Thoughts*. It is true that in this
poem he said,

> Insatiate Archer! could not *One* suffice?
> Thy Shaft flew *thrice*; and *thrice* my Peace was slain;
> And thrice, ere thrice yon Moon had fill'd her Horn,[2]

which would make all three deaths occur within three months,
rather than four years. But in his *Night Thoughts* Young was
not writing his autobiography. *The Complaint or Night
Thoughts* came out in nine books between the years 1742 and
1745. Young wrote only two more works of any importance.
One, *The Centaur not Fabulous*, which has been called 'a kind
of *Night Thoughts* in prose', is a very tedious piece of moralising, interesting only for its most unusual title. It includes,
however, a passage which illustrates well the main theme of the
Night Thoughts and I shall refer to this in due course. The
other work was his critical essay, *Conjectures on Original
Composition*, which is admirably discussed in Logan Pearsall
Smith's *Words and Idioms*.[3] It was the most revolutionary piece
of criticism written in the eighteenth century before the Preface
to the *Lyrical Ballads*. He became very friendly with Samuel
Richardson, an interesting and significant relationship, as
they were the two English writers of the century to have the
greatest influence on the Continent. He visited London
occasionally, and Tunbridge Wells; he carried on a long
correspondence with the Duchess of Portland, of no great
interest.[4] (The Duchess once appeared at a masked ball as

---

[1] Mr Forster has been able to correct the dates given in Shelley of
the deaths in Young's family.

[2] *Night Thoughts: Night First*, 212–14.

[3] *Op. cit.* (1928), 101–6.

[4] *Historical Manuscripts Commission* (1904), I, 254–300.

Cynthia; Young paid her the remarkable compliment of referring to the moon in the *Night Thoughts* as 'fair Portland of the
skies'.) For some reason he quarrelled with his son. He fell
more under the influence of his housekeeper than his friends
liked. He founded Welwyn School and managed its affairs
himself. It must have been one of the first schools in England to
provide military training. In 1758 'a company of honest little
boys educated in loyal principles and generously disclaiming
the conduct of their elder countrymen, formed themselves of
their own accord into a regular Militia, and exercise weekly
under a proper Instructor, to show their zeal and ambition to
serve His Majesty and defend their country'.[1] He tended his
garden. In *The Centaur not Fabulous* he had spoken enthusiastically of gardening. 'What is requisite to make a wise and
happy man, but reflection and peace? and both are the natural
growth of a garden. . . . A garden weeds the mind; it weeds it of
worldly thoughts, and sows celestial seeds in their stead.'
Some years after his death, Boswell and Johnson visited the
house where he had lived. 'We went into the garden, where we
found a gravel walk, on each side of which was a row of trees,
planted by Dr. Young, which formed a handsome Gothick arch;
Dr. Johnson called it a fine grove. I beheld it with reverence.'[2]
Young died on 5 April, 1765. On his deathbed he sent for his
son, but was too ill to see him before he died.

The *Night Thoughts* is divided into nine books, each with its
own title. There is no reason to suppose that Young originally
intended it to be longer than the first four, which came out together. They are comparatively short, just over 2500 lines in
all. The remaining five are longer, and more long-winded,
amounting to over 7000 lines, the ninth and last having over 2400.

The poem opens with the line,

Tir'd Nature's sweet Restorer, balmy *Sleep*!

and critics have often drawn attention to its Shakespearean
quality. Indeed, J. W. Mackail declared that most men, if

---

[1] *A Short History of Welwyn School* (n.d.), 4.
[2] *Boswell's Life of Johnson*, IV, 120.

asked to give its author, would say that it was by Shakespeare.[1] For that matter, it very nearly is. We shall find such echoes, sometimes very close ones, throughout the poem. The most egregious is in the last book,

> While *Chaos* triumphs, repossest of All
> Rival *Creation* ravish'd from his Throne.
> CHAOS! of *Nature* both the Womb, and Grave![2]

Milton, we remember, wrote of

> this wild Abyss
> The womb of Nature and perhaps her grave.[3]

The very last lines of the final book,

> When TIME, like Him of *Gaza* in his Wrath,
> Plucking the Pillars that support the World,
> In NATURE's ample Ruins lies intomb'd;
> And MIDNIGHT, *Universal* Midnight! reigns,

must have been inspired by the close of the *Dunciad*. But, although Young often recalls the verses of his most illustrious forebears and contemporaries, it was not in them that he found the material for his poem.

It often seems to be taken for granted that Young's *Night Thoughts*, whatever else may be said of it, is a highly original poem. It was written by an author who was to claim originality as a great literary virtue; it certainly seemed shatteringly original to writers on the Continent of Europe, especially in Germany. But this judgment needs many reservations. Whatever may be thought of the poetic treatment of Young's ideas, the ideas themselves were not in the least original. In fact, from the point of view of its material, there is no poem in the English language which is more completely conventional than the *Night Thoughts*.

In the poem there meet two English literary traditions, both at that time flowing in full spate, the well-established

---

[1] J. W. Mackail, *Studies of English Poets* (1926), 127.
[2] IX, 1548–50.   [3] *Paradise Lost*, II, 910–11.

poetical tradition of exalting Melancholy and the more recent
outburst of theological writings which resisted atheism, deism
and infidelity generally. A short consideration of these is
essential if we are to understand what Young in his *Night
Thoughts* intended to achieve and if we are to account for its
astonishing success.

The theme of *Memento mori* is one of the commonest in all
literature and it may be expressed in innumerable ways.

> The grave's a fine and private place,
> But none, I think, do there embrace,

is just as sincere an expression of it as a more splendid treatment,

> The glories of our blood and state
> Are shadows, not substantial things.

Behind all descriptions of the transient in Nature or in human
endeavour lies the unspoken conviction, 'It is Margaret you
mourn for.' The more extrovert treatment, the 'Dance of
Death', '*Timor mortis conturbat me*,' the skull and bones, the
charnel house were as familiar in the Middle Ages as in the
eighteenth century. What was peculiar in its development in
English Literature during the fifty years or so before Young's
poem was its ubiquity; it became as natural and easy a subject
for immature or second-rate poets as the love-lyric in the days
of Elizabeth.[1] Horace lost his urbanity and became a mine for
quotations to be used as mottoes for poems on death. The
Arcadian retreat became one, not to a cheerful cottage and a
good day's work, but to surroundings where melancholy might
the more easily call a man for her own. Few were as honest as
Richard Steele in admitting that it might be quite a pleasant
experience, though no doubt many actually enjoyed it.

When we are advanced in years, there is not a more pleasing
entertainment than to recollect in a gloomy moment the
many we have parted with that have been dear and agreeable
to us, and to cast a melancholy thought or two after those

[1] A. L. Reed, *The Background of Gray's Elegy* (New York, 1924).

with whom, perhaps, we have indulged ourselves in whole nights of mirth and jollity. With such inclinations in my heart I went to my closet yesterday in the evening, and resolved to be sorrowful.[1]

A reader in the 1740's who bought a poem entitled *Night Thoughts* would have known exactly what to expect and he would have found what he expected.

Young, then, threw his Thoughts or meditations into the most conventional form he could have found. They occurred at night and they were assisted by the moonlight and the silence. Nor were these meditations themselves the least original. The purpose of the poem is to destroy infidelity. Its essential argument was exactly that which he was to express in the pas sage to which I have referred in *The Centaur not Fabulous*; it may be easily summarised. 'Faith', Young declares, 'is entirely the result of reason;' it is something which can and must be intellectually comprehended. The necessary intellectual effort is prevented by sensual pleasures. These pleasures, of their nature transient, belong to the present. Their lure can be dispelled by a belief in immortality, but infidelity destroys such a belief. Therefore, infidelity is the root of the trouble. To rescue someone from the false pleasures of sense one must, then, restore his belief in immortality. This was not quite all, however. The contemplation of death may make him realise the futility of sensual delights. But, if death is regarded as the end of all things, it may lead rather to the sentiment '*Carpe diem*'. Once more the answer lies in a belief in immortality. That is the essential message which Young wanted to convey and 'Night First' is entitled 'On Life, Death, and Immortality'.

Nothing could have been more completely in tune with the sentiments of his age. Exactly the same points were being made by the Christian apologists of the time in their struggle against the deists and the infidels.[2] To use these

---

[1] *The Tatler*, No. 180 (1710).

[2] I. St. J. Bliss, *Young's Night Thoughts in Relation to Contemporary Christian Apologetics* (Publications of the Modern Language Association of America (1934), XLIX, 37–70.)

writings may well seem to be mere shadow-boxing. There seems to be no evidence of any effective opposition to the secure, stagnant orthodoxy of the English eighteenth-century Church, until one moves into social territory in which Young was not in the least interested, the working-classes in the great cities, the miners of Bristol or Cornwall, to whom Whitfield and John Wesley were preaching. The writers against whom Young was writing, such as Charles Blount, Anthony Collins and John Toland, are wholly forgotten. Certainly when orthodox churchmen in the nineteenth century had to buckle on their armour once more, it was not against them.

There was rather more in the danger, however, than may appear at first sight. For one thing the opponents of orthodox Christianity had behind them great figures who were far from negligible, Thomas Hobbes and John Locke. Also, their approach was not a frontal one, but a flank attack on a side inadequately guarded. Its nature may be summed up in the titles of two of the deist contributions to the controversy, *Christianity not mysterious* by John Toland and *Christianity as Old as the Creation: or, the Gospel a Republication of the Religion of Nature* by Matthew Tindal. Dr Johnson may have called 'the rascal Tindal' an 'atheist', but he would have been much easier to deal with if he had been one. What Tindal did was not to deny the existence of God, but to affirm it, and then to show that human reason could lead one to exactly the same tenets as Christianity, which became something essentially super-fluous. The difficulty was that the orthodox supporters of Christianity were just as anxious to accept the claims of reason. Bishop Sherlock had put it, 'the religion of the Gospel is the true original religion of reason and nature,' and 'declarative of that original religion which was as old as the creation'. 'Faith,' then, as Young said, was 'entirely the result of reason'.

There was nothing, however, of which the orthodox were more frightened than what seemed to them to be the probable results of the new scientific discoveries of the age; few, indeed, were more alarmed than the discoverers themselves. Thus Robert Boyle, a deeply religious man, wrote works of Christian apologetics as well as scientific treatises, and founded in his will eight lectures to be given each year on the evidences of Christianity. Newton, himself, had felt it necessary in his great scientific books to show that his theories should in no way lead men to doubt the existence and omnipotence of God, but rather the reverse. 'For it became him who created them to set them in order.' (He is referring to 'the hard and solid particles' of which 'all material things seem to have been composed, variously associated in the first Creation by the Counsel of an intelligent agent'.)

And if he did so, it's unphilosophical to seek for any other Origin of the World, or to pretend that it might arise out of Chaos by the mere Laws of Nature, though being once form'd, it may continue by those Laws for many Ages. For while Comets move in very excentrick Orbs in all manner of Positions, blind Fate could never make all the Planets move one and the same way in Orbs concentrick, some inconsiderable irregularities excepted, which may have risen from the mutual Actions of Comets and Planets upon one another.[1]

Newton, in fact, seemed to have plugged the leak as soon as it appeared. It was not unnatural that men should at first have been thrown quite off their balance by the new astronomical discoveries, that Donne should exclaim on hearing the news of Galileo's telescope that

'Tis all in pieces, all coherance gone,
All just supply, and all relation,

or that the infinite spaces of the new cosmology should seem to Pascal so terrifying. But Newton removed the confusion and the terror. The mystical mathematics of the City of Heaven were now seen to be — just mathematics. It took a little time for ordinary men to understand and appreciate the work of Newton and the way in which it might be made to redound to the glory of God. But before long the *Principia Mathematica* produced its popularisers and Young leant heavily on one of these, significantly entitled *Astro-theology, or A Demonstration*

[1] Isaac Newton, *Opticks*, Third Edition, corrected (1721), 378.

of the Being and Attributes of God, from a survey of the Heavens,
by the Reverend William Derham. Thus, at the climax of the
last book of his poem, Young could write,

O for a Telescope His Throne to reach!
Tell me, ye Learn'd on *Earth*! or Blest *Above*!
Ye searching, ye *Newtonian* angels! tell,
Where, your Great MASTER's Orb? His Planets, where?
Those *conscious* Satellites, those *Morning-Stars*,
First-born of DEITY! from Central Love,
By Veneration most profound, thrown off;
By sweet Attraction, no less strongly drawn;
Aw'd, and yet *raptur'd*; *raptur'd*, yet *serene*;
Past Thought, illustrious, but with borrow'd Beams;
In still *approaching* Circles, still *remote*,
Revolving round the Sun's eternal SIRE?[1]

The three planetary laws of Kepler could be successfully drawn
into the battle against the sceptic.

Perhaps it was all more than shadow-boxing. Young and the
theologians on whom he relied were writing for a comparatively
small audience. The great mass of the middle- and working-
classes might be quite unaffected by the infidelity which they
were attacking, but the Churchmen were concerned about the
views of a social and political *élite*. Johnson's very obvious fear
of atheism and deism and his own most secret doubts and fears
may show that the danger was more real than one might think.
Montesquieu said of the higher circles of society in England that
'everyone laughs if one talks religion'. And in the background
lay forces far more dangerous — Bayle, the Encyclopaedists
and the great Voltaire. It was they who were to nourish Gibbon
rather than the forgotten English theological controversialists
of Young's day.

Young, then, in his *Night Thoughts* uses a completely conventional form, that of the poetry of Melancholy and Night,
to treat a completely conventional subject, the defence of the
revealed Christian religion against infidelity. But a conventional
theme treated in a conventional way may yet be written in an

[1] IX, 1834–5.

original manner. To see whether this can be claimed for Young we must consider the poem itself.

It is possible to trace an evolution in its course. In the first three Nights Lorenzo, who in the later books is to be the man of the world at whom Young's teaching is directed, plays a comparatively small part. The last four books are much more obviously didactic than the earlier ones. Young at first is trying to convince himself. Night, with its conventional attributes, turns his mind toward death and in particular the deaths of Philander, his friend, who is usually assumed to be Henry Temple, and, in the third book, of Narcissa, who is his stepdaughter. The fact of immortality is more or less taken for granted; the lessons to be learnt are those which human mortality teaches us. Young's first purpose is to persuade his reader to face the fact of the inevitability of death.

The opening contains a description of Night, which must surely be accounted one of the finest passages in the poetry of the school to which Young belonged.

> *Night*, sable Goddess! from her *Ebon* Throne,
> In rayless Majesty, now stretches forth
> Her leaden Sceptre o'er a slumb'ring World.
> Silence, how dead! And Darkness, how profound!
> Nor Eye, nor list'ning Ear, an Object finds;
> Creation sleeps. 'Tis as the gen'ral Pulse
> Of Life stood still, and Nature made a Pause,
> An aweful Pause! prophetic of her End.
> And let the Prophecy be soon fulfill'd;
> *Fate!* drop the Curtain; I can lose no more.[1]

It may be worth our while to consider these lines for a moment. The blank verse, remarkably well controlled from the start, certainly owes something to Milton. (Young would have been unique among English writers of blank verse in the eighteenth century if it had not.) But it is not merely Miltonic. The rhythm is a great deal more staccato; the structure of the sentences constantly emphasises the caesura. We may notice

[1] *The Complaint: or, Night-Thoughts on Life, Death, and Immortality. A New Edition, Corrected by the Author* (1756), p. 2, I, 18–27.

the proliferation of exclamation marks, though what he does in this passage is nothing to what he could show himself capable of, and also how much of the work is done by epithets, some of them a good deal too inevitable, 'sable goddess', 'ebon throne', 'leaden sceptre', 'slumb'ring world'. On the other hand, he knew well how to make an effect by dramatically simplifying his language in contrast,

> Creation sleeps. 'Tis as the gen'ral Pulse
> Of Life stood still, and Nature made a Pause.

His style, in fact, is a highly rhetorical one, and it has all the weaknesses of rhetorical verse. When inspiration flags, the rhetoric will carry him on for lines which sometimes become practically incomprehensible. I have some sympathy with John Wesley, who found it necessary, when including passages from the *Night Thoughts* in an anthology of religious verse, to correct many of the lines and explain the hard words, 'in order to make that noble work more useful to all and more intelligible to ordinary readers'.[1] Young, indeed, often became very long-winded. On the other hand, he had a gift for the concentrated phrase. The following passage shows him both at his most verbose and at his most effective. Lorenzo, the man of the world, has claimed that Death

> marks his Way
> With dreadful Waste of what deserves to shine!
> Art, Genius, Fortune, elevated Power!
> With various Lustres *These* light up the World,
> Which *Death* puts out, and darkens human Race.

This is an important point in the argument of the poem. Young has now to demonstrate a paradox, that life, because it is of necessity transient, is mortal, while death, because it opens the gate to eternal life, should be regarded as immortal.

> I grant, LORENZO! this Indictment just:
> The Sage, Peer, Potentate, King, Conqueror!
> *Death* humbles These; more barb'rous *Life*, the *Man*.

[1] John Wesley, *Journals* (20 December, 1768).

The list in the second line is almost wholly tautologous. As he proceeds he begins to repeat himself, making his case no stronger by doing so, and then he saves the situation by producing in the last sentence an epigram of undoubted power.

> *Life* is the Triumph of our mould'ring Clay;
> *Death*, of the Spirit infinite! divine!
> *Death* has no Dread, but what frail *Life* imparts;
> Nor *Life* true Joy, but what kind *Death* improves.
> No Bliss has *Life* to boast, till Death can give
> Far greater; *Life's* a Debtor to the Grave,
> Dark Lattice! letting in eternal Day.[1]

In a famous passage in the first book Young deals with the theme that man is incapable of accepting the fact of death. It begins with the surprising lines,

> Beware, LORENZO! a *slow-sudden* Death.
> How dreadful that deliberate Surprize!

I think the paradox is justified and that the lines that follow explain it.

> Be wise To-day; 'tis Madness to defer;
> Next Day the fatal Precedent will plead;
> Thus on, till Wisdom is push'd out of Life.
> *Procrastination* is the Thief of Time;
> Year after Year it steals, till all are fled,
> And to the Mercies of a Moment leaves
> The vast Concerns of an eternal Scene.
> If not so frequent, would not This be strange?
> That 'tis so frequent, *This* is stranger still.
> Of Man's miraculous Mistakes, this bears
> The Palm, 'That all Men are about to live,'
> For ever on the Brink of being born.

And then, after a few lines more, he sums it up,

> All *Promise* is poor dilatory Man,
> And that thro' ev'ry Stage: When young, indeed,
> In full Content, we, sometimes, nobly rest,

[1] P. 66, III, 459–73.

Un-anxious for *ourselves*; and only wish,
As duteous Sons, our Fathers were more wise.
At *Thirty* Man *suspects* himself a Fool;
Knows it at *Forty*, and reforms his Plan;
At *Fifty* chides his infamous Delay,
Pushes his prudent Purpose to *Resolve*;
In all the Magnanimity of Thought
Resolves; and re-resolves; then dies the same.
And why? Because he thinks himself immortal.
All Men think all Men mortal, but Themselves.[1]

Quite apart from the well-known proverbial line,

Procrastination is the Thief of Time,

(which most people think has something to do with the normal
casualness of life, but that was not the kind of thing Young
was interested in) this is a very skilful piece of writing.

In the third book Young turns to the death of Narcissa, who
is usually taken to be his step-daughter, and, as she dies
abroad, this is no doubt right.

With Haste, parental Haste,
I flew, I snatch'd her from the rigid North,
Her native Bed, on which black *Boreas* blew,
And bore her nearer to the Sun.[2]

He proceeds to give a very hysterical description of her burial.
It is clear that what he means is that she was denied a grave
in a Christian cemetery because she was a Protestant.

For Oh! the curst Ungodliness of Zeal!
While *sinful Flesh* relented, *Spirit* nurst
In blind *Infallibility's* Embrace,
The *Sainted Spirit* petrify'd the Breast;
Deny'd the Charity of Dust, to spread
O'er Dust! a Charity their Dogs enjoy.
What could I do? What Succour? What Resource?
With pious Sacrilege, a Grave I stole;
With impious Piety that Grave I wrong'd;

[1] Pp. 16–17, I, 389–425.   [2] Pp. 52–3, III, 116–19.

Short in my Duty; Coward in my Grief!
More like her Murderer, than Friend, I crept,
With soft-suspended Step; and, muffled deep
In midnight Darkness, *whisper'd* my Last Sigh.
I *whisper'd* what should echo thro' their Realms;
Nor writ her Name, whose Tomb should pierce the Skies.
Presumptuous Fear! How durst I dread her Foes,
While Nature's loudest Dictates I obey'd?
Pardon Necessity, Blest Shade! Of Grief
And Indignation rival Bursts I pour'd;
Half-execration mingled with my Pray'r;
Kindled at Man, while I his God ador'd!
Sore-grudg'd the Savage Land her Sacred Dust;
Stampt the curst Soil; and with Humanity
(Deny'd NARCISSA) wisht them all a Grave.[1]

When, before long, the *Night Thoughts* were translated into
French and swept the country, France stood appalled at this
picture of her intolerance and insensitivity. Unfortunately for
Young's reputation, however, investigations carried out at
Lyons in 1835 showed that the body of Mrs Temple had been
decently buried — at night, it is true, but that was customary
with Protestant burials — in the Swiss cemetery of the town.
Moreover, far from Young being unable to write her name, her
tomb was covered with a slab of black marble, on which was
carved a long inscription in Latin, giving her name, with full
details of her illustrious descent from King Charles II.[2]

Are we to take this as evidence of Young's 'radical insincerity', to use George Eliot's phrase about him? I do not think
that he need be condemned so completely. Narcissa was no
doubt Elizabeth Temple, and Philander was, in all probability,
her husband. But in the poem Narcissa dies soon after Philander, not four years before. Young was not writing an
accurate narrative. No doubt the three deaths of those dear to

[1] Pp. 54–5, III, 165–88.
[2] Joseph Texte, *Jean-Jacques Rousseau et les Origines du Cos-
mopolitisme Littéraire* (Paris, 1895), 371. W. Thomas, *Le Poète Edward
Young*, 137–9.

him were the immediate cause of the poem, but he hid their
personalities in obviously fictitious names and he felt no com-
punction in altering the facts for his own dramatic purposes.
There can be no doubt that he borrowed the idea from Pope's
Elegy to the Memory of an Unfortunate Lady, who also died in a
foreign land and was also refused a Christian burial, though in
her case it was because she had committed suicide. Still,
Narcissa was Elizabeth Temple, and Young's narrative here
comes very near the facts. 'Radical insincerity' may be too
severe a judgment, but Young at this point showed very
questionable taste. The truth was that he thoroughly disliked
the French. 'As we are at War with the Power, it were as well
if we were at War with the Manners, of France,' he wrote in
1744. 'A Land of *Levity*, is a Land of *Guilt*.[1] The French paid
him back very generously for this insult.[2]

In the fourth book the poem becomes more didactic and
Young is now engaged in the attempt to convert Lorenzo.
Although in the remaining books he occasionally speaks of the
views he held as Christian, it is only here that he dwells at any
length on the Christian revelation, the Crucifixion and the
Resurrection. I think it is worth while to analyse a part of this
book; it throws a remarkable light on the religion of Young's
day.

> And did He rise?
> Hear, O ye Nations! hear it, O ye Dead!
> He rose! He rose! He burst the Bars of Death.

[1] *Night Thoughts*, VII, Preface.

[2] Young is still remembered in France. The *Michelin Guide* to
Gorges du Tarn, Cévennes, Bas Languedoc refers to the so-called
Tombeau de Narcissa in the Jardin des Plantes at Montpellier. 'On
raconte qu'à la fin du 18e s. le poète anglais Arthur (sic) Young vint à
Montpellier pour essayer de sauver sa fille Narcissa, atteinte de con-
somption. Le climat, malgré sa douceur, ne put que retarder l'issue
fatale. Le poète fit enterrer la jeune fille dans le beau jardin où elle
aimait venir se reposer.' Hardly a word in the account is correct, but
what a tribute to the poet who has been forgotten by his own country!
It was by the 'tombeau de Narcissa' that Paul Valéry, as a young man,
used to foregather with his friends, André Gide and Pierre Louÿs.

　　　Lift up your Heads, ye everlasting Gates!
　　　And give the King of Glory to come in:
　　　Who is the King of Glory? He who left
　　　His Throne of Glory, for the Pang of Death:
　　　Lift up your Heads, ye everlasting Gates!
　　　And give the King of Glory to come in.
　　　Who is the King of Glory? He who slew
　　　The rav'nous Foe, that gorg'd all human Race!
　　　The King of Glory, He, whose Glory fill'd
　　　Heav'n with Amazement at his Love to Man;
　　　And with Divine Complacency beheld
　　　Powr's most illumin'd, wilder'd in the Theme.[1]

Sustained by the psalmist, and by Milton, Young for some
time rhapsodises on the theme. But in the end we are told that
the truth could apparently be discovered without this stupen-
dous demonstration by God.

　　　To Man the bleeding Cross has promis'd *All*;
　　　The bleeding Cross has sworn eternal Grace;
　　　Who gave his Life, what Grace shall He deny?
　　　O ye! who, from this *Rock of Ages*, leap,
　　　Disdainful, plunging headlong in the Deep![2]

　　These lines were written thirty years before Toplady's hymn.
Young may have found the now so familiar phrase in the
marginal rendering of Isaiah, 'In the Lord Jehovah is the
Rock of Ages'.[3] But he could never have added,

　　　　　　Simply to thy Cross I cling,

for within a very few lines the mystery of the Redemption is
seen in a very different light.

　　　The Beam dim *Reason* sheds shows Wonders there:
　　　What high Contents! Illustrious Faculties!
　　　But the grand *Comment*, which displays at Full
　　　Our human Height, scarce sever'd from Divine,
　　　By Heav'n composed, was publish'd on the Cross.[4]

[1] P. 81, IV, 271–85.　　　　　[2] Pp. 88–9, IV, 474–8.
[3] Isaiah XXVI, 4.　　　　　　[4] P. 89, IV, 489–93.

'The *grand comment*' — it was all very well for Young then to declare 'Religion's all', and to exclaim,

> *Religion!* thou the Soul of Happiness;
> And, groaning *Calvary*, of thee! *There* shine
> The noblest Truths; *there* strongest Motives sting;
> There sacred Violence assaults the Soul;
> There, nothing but *Compulsion* is forborn.[1]

Calvary and the Resurrection are, in fact, to be relegated to an explanatory note. Lorenzo must be converted by other arguments.

> Read Nature; Nature is a Friend to Truth;
> Nature is Christian; preaches to Mankind;
> And bids dead Matter aid us in our Creed.[2]

In a splendid passage he brings up Halley in support with his demonstration of the punctual return of the comets. They are more convincing evidence than the Christian revelation.

> Hast thou ne'er seen the Comet's flaming Flight?
> Th'illustrious Stranger passing, Terror sheds
> On gazing Nations, from his fiery Train
> Of Length enormous, takes his ample Round
> Thro' Depths of Ether; coasts unnumber'd Worlds,
> Of more than solar Glory; doubles wide
> Heav'n's mighty Cape; and then revisits Earth,
> From the long Travel of a thousand Years.
> Thus, at the destin'd Period, shall return
> HE, once on Earth, who bids the Comet blaze:
> And, with Him, all our Triumph o'er the Tomb.[3]

It would still seem, however, that Reason is not capable of solving the mystery of life to come.

> *Nature* is dumb on this important Point;
> Or Hope precarious in low Whisper breathes;
> *Faith* speaks aloud, distinct; even *Adders* hear,
> But turn, and dart into the Dark again.
> *Faith* builds a Bridge across the Gulph of Death,

[1] P. 92, IV, 575–9.   [2] P. 97, IV, 703–5.   [3] Pp. 97–8, IV, 706–16.

G

> To break the Shock blind *Nature* cannot shun,
> And lands Thought smoothly on the farther Shore.
> Death's Terror is the Mountain *Faith* removes;
> That Mountain Barrier between Man and Peace.
> 'Tis *Faith* disarms Destruction; and absolves
> From ev'ry clam'rous Charge, the guiltless Tomb.
> Why disbelieve; LORENZO!

But Lorenzo is not satisfied and sticks to his guns.

>   '*Reason* bids,
>   All-sacred Reason.'

The answer comes immediately, and with it Revelation is finally relegated to the background.

>   — Hold her sacred still;
> Nor shalt thou want a Rival in thy Flame:
> All-sacred *Reason*! Source, and Soul, of all
> Demanding Praise, on Earth, or Earth above!
> My Heart is thine.[1]

Lorenzo reiterates,

>   'On Argument alone my Faith is built,'

only to find again that his plea is at once accepted.

> *Reason* pursu'd is *Faith*; and, unpursu'd
> Where Proof invites, 'tis Reason, then, no more:
> And such our *Proof*, That, or our *Faith* is *right*,
> Or *Reason* lyes, and Heav'n design'd it *wrong*:
> Absolve we This? What, then, is Blasphemy?
> Fond as we are, and justly fond of *Faith*,
> *Reason*, we grant, demands our first Regard;
> The Mother honour'd, as the Daughter dear.
> *Reason* the Root; fair *Faith* is but the Flower;
> The fading Flow'r shall die; but *Reason* lives
> Immortal, as her Father in the Skies.[2]

'The fading Flow'r shall die.' That is what the Christian revelation comes to in the end. We can hardly avoid hearing an echo in these lines. Reason, we feel, has taken the place of Charity.

[1] P. 98, IV, 717–33.   [2] P. 99, IV, 742–53.

With that the poem originally ended. The 'Fifth Night', which came out in the following year, does little to advance the argument. There are the same encomiums of Night,

> Night is fair Virtue's immemorial Friend;
> The conscious Moon, thro' every distant Age,
> Has held a Lamp to *Wisdom*, and let fall,
> On *Contemplation's* Eye, her purging Ray,[1]

the same insistence on the ever-present reality of death. Young is one of the most repetitive of poets and yet his control of his verse is sure enough to make us feel that we are being moved along the whole time.

In October 1743 Young wrote to the Duchess of Portland for the loan of 'Bishop Gastrell's work'. This was *Moral Proofs of the Certainty of a Future State*, which had been published in 1725. It plays a large part in the next two 'Nights', the sixth and seventh, which appeared in 1745. In a new preface to these Young declares that the whole dispute about religion 'may be reduced to this single Question, Is Man Immortal, or is he not? If he is not, all our Disputes are mere Amusements, or Trials of Skill'. He is determined to fight the battle on the ground of his opponent's choice. 'The sacred Page assures us, that Life and Immortality[2] are brought to Light by the Gospel; but by how many is the Gospel rejected, or overlooked! . . . Here, therefore, in Proof of this most fundamental Truth (that of the immortality of the soul), some plain Arguments are offered, Arguments derived from Principles which Infidels admit in common with Believers.' The Bishop had said exactly the same in his own preface. But Young was writing poetry. He found in the *Moral Proof*, for instance — he used other books as well[3] — the argument that the regular cycle of nights and days and of

---

[1] P. 111, V, 177–80.

[2] I note a delightful misprint in the 1758 edition, 'Immorality'.

[3] I. St.J. Bliss, *op. cit.* (Miss Bliss shows that Young seems to have made no use of Butler's *Analogy of Religion*, and in an interesting note points out that this great work, published in 1736, received remarkably little attention for some years after it first appeared (p. 63).)

the seasons points to a similar everlastingness in the soul of man, but a reader interested in theological discussion would not find such language as this in the Bishop's earnest pages:

> Look Nature thro', 'tis *Revolution* all;
> All Change, no Death. Day follows Night; and Night
> The dying Day; Stars rise, and set, and rise;
> Earth takes th' Example. See, the *Summer* gay,
> With her green Chaplet, and ambrosial Flowers,
> Droops into pallid *Autumn*: *Winter* grey,
> Horrid with Frost, and turbulent with Storm,
> Blows *Autumn*, and his golden Fruits, away:
> Then melts into the *Spring*: Soft *Spring*, with Breath
> *Favonian*, from warm Chambers of the South,
> Recalls the *First*. All, to reflourish, fades.
> As in a Wheel, All sinks, to reascend.
> Emblems of Man, who passes, not expires.[1]

It is interesting to compare this passage with one on exactly the same theme in James Thomson's *Winter*.[2] I should not hesitate to claim that *The Seasons* is a greater poem than *Night Thoughts*, but here I think Young is certainly more exciting and his lines are free from the insufferable complacency of Thomson's treatment of the argument. It can hardly be called a convincing one. It all depends on how you look at it, either 'All change; no death' or, as Young himself had written in his play, *The Revenge*,

> Day buries day; month, month, and year the year:
> Our life is but a chain of many deaths.

It is hardly necessary to dwell on the other arguments Young uses: that, if matter is immortal and

> No single Atom, once in Being, lost,[3]

how much more so must be the spirit; that the architectural and engineering achievements of Man,

> What levell'd Mountains! and what lifted Vales!
> O'er Vales and Mountains sumptuous Cities swell,[4]

[1] P. 175, VI, 677–89.   [2] *The Seasons*, 'Winter', 1024–69.
[3] P. 176, VI, 699.   [4] P. 179, VI, 771–2.

point to the work of an immortal being,

> Whose Footsteps These ? — *Immortals* have been Here.
> Could *less* than Souls Immortal this have done ?[1]

The arguments follow thick and fast, but Young's rhetoric, his paradoxes and antitheses, are capable of adorning them all. Man's discontent argues that he cannot find his goal in this life. His constant desire for more, his hope, looking always to the future, are evidence of his immortal nature.

He tackles the works of Shaftesbury and Francis Hutcheson with their seductive theories of disinterested benevolence and the 'natural' affections which lead men to virtuous actions without thought of reward. The orthodox theologians looked on these writers with particular suspicion and perhaps they were right, for their views pointed directly to Utilitarianism. Hutcheson himself used the phrase, 'the greatest happiness for the greatest numbers.' But if, on the contrary, self-interest is the law of man's being, then virtue would be sensible only if it could be rewarded and vice punished in a future life, and so the ideal of disinterested virtue,

> The rigid Guardian of a blameless Heart,
> So long rever'd, so long reputed wise,
> Is weak; with rank Knight-errantries o'er-run.
> Why beats thy Bosom with illustrious Dreams
> Of Self-exposure, laudable, and great?
> Of gallant Enterprize, and glorious Death?
> Die for thy country? — Thou Romantic Fool!
> Seize, seize the Plank thyself, and let her sink:
> Thy *Country*! what to Thee? — The *Godhead*; what?
> (I speak with Awe!) tho' He should bid thee bleed?
> If, with thy Blood, thy *final* Hope is spilt,
> Nor can Omnipotence reward the Blow,
> Be deaf; preserve thy Being; disobey.
> Nor is it Disobedience: Know, LORENZO!
> Whate'er th' ALMIGHTY's subsequent Command,
> His first Command is *this*: — 'Man, love thyself.'[2]

[1] P. 180, VI, 804–5.   [2] P. 192, VII, 155–70.

It must be admitted that all this is put much more excitingly than in the works of the theological controversialists of the time.

It is not necessary to follow Young's arguments further. He is engaged in showing that a belief in immortality alone makes sense of man's nature,

> 'Tis *Immortality* decyphers Man,
> And opens all the Myst'ries of his Make.
> Without it, half his *Instincts* are a Riddle;
> Without it, all his *Virtues* are a Dream.[1]

Young was to add two more 'Nights', which appeared in the following year. 'Night Eighth' does little to advance the argument, and the pictures of the miseries of a vicious life and the advantages of virtue are, on the whole, conventional. But in the last night, the 'Ninth', he returns to a theme he has touched on occasionally before, the evidence of the celestial order. Here his verse sometimes attains a real splendour.

> LORENZO! such the Glories of the World?
> What is the World itself? *Thy* World — A Grave.
> Where is the Dust that has not been alive?
> The Spade, the Plough, disturb our Ancestors;
> From human Mould we reap our daily Bread.
> The Globe around Earth's hollow Surface shakes,
> And is the Ceiling of her sleeping Sons.
> O'er Devastation we blind Revels keep;
> Whole bury'd Towns support the Dancer's Heel.[2]

From earth, with the guidance of Newton's laws and his theological interpretation of them, we must rise to the stars. He calls on Lorenzo to begin a 'Tour thro' *Nature's* universal Orb'.[3] He invoked 'Heaven's king, who didst touch the lip of Jesse's son', to inspire him.

> Teach me, by this stupendous Scaffolding,
> Creation's golden Steps, to climb to THEE.[4]

[1] P. 205, VII, 507–10.   [2] P. 304, IX, 90–8.
[3] P. 324, IX, 609.   [4] P. 323, IX, 580–93.

No one before Young had written so enthusiastically of the
stars and planets moving in their Newtonian dance. His theme
was far from original. Addison, whom he revered, had fore-
shadowed a whole school of poetry in his famous hymn, though,
strangely enough, his picture of the Universe was pre-
Copernican. Young echoed him when he wrote,

> Bright Legions swarm unseen, and sing, unheard
> By mortal Ear, the glorious Architect,
> In This His universal Temple, hung
> With Lustres, with innumerable Lights.[1]

He might assault his readers with the question,

> And dare *Earth's* bold Inhabitants deny
> The sumptuous, the magnific Embassy
> A Moment's Audience ?[2]

The poets of the time were making it very difficult for earth's
inhabitants to do so, and Newton,

> pure Intelligence, whom God
> To mortals lent,[3]

as James Thomson described him, was generally accepted as
the spokesman of the embassy. Readers of the *Night Thoughts*
were not being asked to make any great effort of mind when
adjured by Young to

> Mark
> The *Mathematic* Glories of the Skies,
> In Number, Weight and Measure, All ordain'd.[4]

What was remarkable was the way in which Young wedded
the visual and the mathematic glories.

> Nor think thou seest a wild Disorder here;
> Thro' this illustrious Chaos to the Sight,
> Arrangement neat, and chastest Order, reign.
> The Path prescrib'd, inviolably kept,
> Upbraids the lawless Sallies of Mankind.
> Worlds, ever thwarting, never interfere;

[1] P. 330, IX, 765–8.   [2] P. 333, IX, 853–8.
[3] *The Seasons*, 'Summer', 1560, I.   [4] P. 342, IX, 1079–81.

What Knots are ty'd! How soon are they dissolv'd,
And yet the seeming marry'd Planets free!
They rove for ever, without Error rove . . .
            On yon cœrulean Plain,
In Exultation to *Their* GOD, and *Thine*,
They dance, they sing eternal Jubilee,
Eternal Celebration of His Praise . . .
Mark, how the *Labyrinthian* Turns they take,
The Circles intricate, and mystic Maze,
Weave the grand Cypher of *Omnipotence*;
To *Gods*, how Great! how Legible to *Man*![1]

Newton had seen as the most remarkable proof of the divine
ordering of the heavens the mysterious fact that all the
elements in the solar system did not rush in towards the
centre,[2] and Young had this no doubt in mind, when he wrote,

Where are the Pillars that support the Skies?
What More than *Atlantean* Shoulder props
Th' incumbent Load? What Magic, what strange Art,
In fluid Air these pond'rous Orbs sustains?[3]

No wonder Young felt he could say,

And yet LORENZO calls for Miracles,
To give his tott'ring Faith a solid Base.
Why call for less than is *already* thine? . . .
            The *Brute*, indeed,
Sees nought but *Spangles* here; the *Fool*, no more.
Say'st thou, 'The Course of *Nature* governs All?'
The *Course* of *Nature* is the *Art* of GOD.
The Miracles thou call'st for, *This* attest;
For say, Could *Nature Nature*'s Course controul?[4]

Newton, as we now realise well enough, was profoundly
altering man's view of God's place in the Universe, but Young,
no more than Newton, was aware of the revolution that had

---

[1] Pp. 343–4, IX, 1108–16; 1124–34.
[2] E. A. Burtt, *The Metaphysical Foundations of Modern Physical Science* (1925), 291.
[3] P. 344, IX, 1136–9.   [4] Pp. 348–9, IX, 1240–2; 1266–71.

taken place. He was content to find evidence for the existence
of God in Design,

> Much Design
> Is seen in all their *Motions*, all their *Makes*;
> *Design* implies *Intelligence*, and *Art*:
> *That* can't be from *Themselves* — or *Man*.[1]

God's work, then, was to set the dance going.

> What Hand behind the Scene,
> What Arm Almighty, put these wheeling Globes
> In Motion, and wound up the vast Machine?[2]

The result was inevitably to turn God into a master mathematician. Young has to grope for titles for the Deity which will
express a new conception of Him. Early in the poem he had at
least styled God 'the great Philanthropist', but now he becomes in turn 'the great Economist', 'the great Artist', 'the
Divine Instructor', 'the great Proprietor' and 'the Illustrious
Mind'. (It might be claimed, however, that Thomson's title for
God, 'informer of the planetary train', goes one better.) He
makes a desperate, but inevitably ridiculous, attempt to link
the Christ of the Gospels with the Newtonian Deity,

> Great VINE! on THEE, on THEE the Cluster hangs;
> The Filial Cluster! infinitely spread
> In glowing Globes.[3]

In the end he consciously wrestles with the problem.

> How shall I name THEE? How my labouring Soul
> Heaves underneath the Thought, too big for Birth!

The answer is remarkable.

> Great System of Perfections! Mighty Cause
> Of Causes mighty! Cause uncaus'd! Sole Root
> Of *Nature*, that luxuriant Growth of GOD!
> First Father of *Effects*! that Progeny
> Of endless Series . . .

[1] P. 357, IX, 1462–5.   [2] P. 349–50, IX, 1275–7.
[3] P. 374, IX, 1914–16.

Father of this immeasurable Mass
Of *Matter* multiform; or dense, or rare;
Opaque, or lucid; rapid, or at Rest,
Minute, or passing Bound![1]

But he was only echoing in language, highly rhetorical, and
sometimes, I think, poetic, the astonishing statement of his
master, Newton, who, after considering the motions of the
planets, the quantities of matter in them, and 'the gravitating
powers resulting from thence', decided that 'to compare and
adjust all these things together in so great a variety of bodies,
argues that cause to be not blind and fortuitous, but very well
skilled in mechanics and geometry'.[2]

It is not difficult to understand why Young's poem was so
popular. He was dealing with problems which much exercised
the men of his time. And he did this in a way which was very
exciting. For there is something original in Young's style.
J. W. Mackail compared his verse to Georgian architecture.[3] I
can imagine no illustration more inadequate. Here was no
repose; if there was certainty, one could see the certainty
being fought for. Young in his *Night Thoughts* is long-winded,
verbose, sometimes obscure, not because the thought is profound, but because he is striving for effect, but the verse moves
onward and carries one with it. Edmund Gosse in his *Father
and Son* spoke of 'the vigour and forward push of Young's
style'. Johnson once read Thomson's poetry aloud to an
admirer; 'and then asked, — Is not this fine? Shiels having expressed the highest admiration. Well, Sir, (said I,) I have omitted
every other line.'[4] Repetitive as Young is, I do not believe that
the experiment would have succeeded with *Night Thoughts*.

The poem was revolutionary. The fact that the matter was
so ordinary, that Young had no ideas or insights that were
not the commonplaces of his own time, only meant that the
revolution was more successful. It caused the poem to be read

---

[1] P. 386, IX, 2215–29.

[2] *Isaaci Newtoni Opera*, ed. S. Horsley (1779–85), IV, 4, quoted in
E. A. Burtt, *op. cit.*, 286.

[3] J. W. Mackail, *op. cit.*, 129.   [4] Boswell's *Life of Johnson*, III, 37.

by thousands. His vigour, his 'hammering on the keys', (to quote J. W. Mackail again, and here his illustration could hardly be bettered) broke up, as it were, the smooth surface of Augustan poetry. His fame abroad, on the other hand, was partly fortuitous. He did not, like his friend Samuel Richardson, who shared his popularity on the Continent, open men's eyes to new vistas in literature and in the understanding of human nature. What impressed the young Frenchmen and Germans of the second half of the eighteenth century was his melancholy; they did not realise how conventional it was in his own country. Young was the poet of death and human wretchedness, '*le sépulchral Young*'. His French translator said that the *Night Thoughts* was 'the most sublime elegy ever written on the miseries of human life'.[1] That was not what Young had intended it to be. When Camille Desmoulins read the poem as he awaited the guillotine, a friend exclaimed, '*Tu veux mourir donc deux fois?*'[2] The poem had a great influence in Germany. Klopstock said that he read the Psalms, the Prophets and the *Night Thoughts* to gain inspiration while writing his epic, *Messias*.[3] It is not surprising that Frau Klopstock was astonished to discover that Young was not Archbishop of Canterbury.[4] More important was its effect on the *Sturm und Drang*. Herder was more influenced by Young's *Original Conjectures* than by the poem, but he wrote of the *Night Thoughts* as 'the *non plus ultra* of ingenious, witty, elevated and pious thoughts, sparkling like the night skies'.[5] In his *Dichtung und Wahrheit* Goethe spoke of the impression it had made on him in the days when he was writing *Werther*.[6] In 1755 William Mason wrote to Gray, describing how he had met in Hamburg a formidable blue-stocking, 'Madame Belcht'.

She asked me who was the famous poet that writ the Nitt toats. I replied Doctr Yonge. She begd leave to drink his

[1] J. Texte, *op. cit.*, 372.   [2] W. Thomas, *op. cit.*, 539.
[3] L. M. Price, *op. cit.*, 114.   [4] H. C. Shelley, *op. cit.*, 247.
[5] L. M. Price, *op. cit.*, 118.
[6] J. Boyd, *Goethe's Knowledge of English Literature* (1932), 141.

Health in a Glass of sweet wine adding that he was her favrite English Author. We toasted the Doctor. Upon wch having a mind to give a Parnassian Toast, I asked Madame Belch if she had ever read La Petite Elegie dans La Cœmeterie Rustique. C'est Beaucoup Jolie je vous Assure! ... Oui, Monsr (replyd Madame Belch) Je lu, & elle est bien Jolie & Melancholique mais elle ne touche point La Cœur comme mes tres chers Nitt toats.[1]

The 'Nitt toats' will not touch our hearts as *La Petite Elegie* still does. For one thing it is a great deal too long and its chief weakness is its complete lack of any comprehensive design. It deals too directly with the controversies of its own time; the doubts created by John Toland or Matthew Tindal are not those that disturb us. Perhaps it will irritate us less than it did the critics of the nineteenth century. We shall not be likely to feel that Young is speaking to us; we can more easily appreciate that he was speaking to his own contemporaries. A humanitarian age, which confidently believed in an active virtue, could hardly fail to be annoyed by Young. He certainly showed no interest in practical Christianity. I know of nowhere in all critical literature where the critic seems to be so totally removed from the work under consideration as George Eliot's essay on the *Night Thoughts*, significantly entitled *Worldliness and Other-Worldliness*.[2] 'Place him on a breezy common, where the furze is in its golden bloom, where children are playing, and horses standing with fondling necks, and he would have nothing to say.' In the face of such heartiness Young would indeed be silent.

What is needed first, when considering a poem that is no longer read, is to discover why the poet wrote it. The great strength of Young's *Night Thoughts* is that it convinces us that he was impelled to write it. In spite of all the shallow philosophising, the commonplace 'astro-theology', I can well believe Young when he said once that he really did compose

[1] *Correspondence of Thomas Gray*, ed. Paget Toynbee and L. Whibley (1935), I, 423–4.

[2] *Blackwood's Magazine* (1857).

most of his poetry at night. For all its rhetoric and garrulity, there is to be found in the poem precisely what George Eliot denied it, 'genuine emotion'. Its place in the history of English Literature seems to be assured. I think it deserves more than that. It is a poem which should still be read.

IV

William Robertson
The History of the Reign of Charles V

'I T is natural to believe . . . that no writer has a more easy task
than the historian. The philosopher has the works of omni-
science to examine; and is therefore engaged in disquisitions, to
which finite intellects are utterly unequal. The poet trusts to
his invention, and is not only in danger of those inconsistencies,
to which every one is exposed by departure from truth; but may
be censured as well for deficiencies of matter, as for irregularity
of disposition, or impropriety of ornament. But the happy
historian has no other labour than of gathering what tradition
pours down before him, or records treasure for his use. He has
only the actions and designs of men like himself to conceive
and to relate; he is not to form, but copy characters.'[1]

Thus Doctor Johnson wrote in *The Rambler* in May 1751.
Twelve years later, dining with Goldsmith and some others, all
Boswell's guests, at the Mitre Tavern, he spoke on the same
subject.

Great abilities are not requisite for an Historian; for in
historical composition, all the greatest powers of the human
mind are quiescent. He has facts ready to his hand; so there is
no exercise of invention. Imagination is not required in any
high degree; only about as much as is used in the lower kinds
of poetry. Some penetration, accuracy, and colouring will fit
a man for the task, if he can give the application which is
necessary.[2]

[1] *The Rambler*, No. 122.   [2] Boswell's *Life of Johnson*, I, 424, 5.

During those twelve years David Hume had published, between 1754 and 1762, his *History of England*; in 1756 had
appeared the *Essai sur l'histoire générale et sur les Mœurs* of
Voltaire; and in 1759 the *History of Scotland* by Dr William
Robertson of Edinburgh. A great revolution had taken place.
When we consider the vast number of historical works which
are published now and have been for several generations, it
might be argued that of all the literary revolutions during the
last two centuries none has influenced more books — except
the one created by Samuel Richardson, whose *Pamela* and
Clarissa appeared between 1740 and 1751. Dr Johnson was
completely unaware of it. This revolution was continued by
Robertson's later histories and by Gibbon's *Decline and Fall*.
It was soon followed by a second revolution in historical writing,
an upheaval which was to bury all the histories written in the
previous half-century — but one. Wolf with his *Prolegomena
to Homer* and Niebuhr in his Lectures at Berlin made it necessary to rewrite classical history; Ranke did the same service for
the history of Modern Europe, burying, among other books, the
History of the Reign of Charles V by William Robertson, which
I shall be considering. Of the Homeric age nothing is left but
Homer; of the great generation of historians to which I have
referred, nothing but Gibbon.

Nor, for that matter, do more than a few experts to-day read
Wolf or Niebuhr or even Ranke. The historian seeking immortality is at a great disadvantage. His works may continue
to be read for the style, though very few books go on being read
for their style alone, or, perhaps, because, being a narrative of
their author's own day, they are regarded as a contemporary
source. But the reader is not satisfied if the work is felt to be
untrue or — and here lies the greatest difficulty — incomplete.

The more one considers how very few historical works are
read for very long, the more one is astonished at the triumph
of Gibbon. We can speak of the adamant of Gibbon. If so, that
alone should make it impossible to ignore Robertson. No
historian, except when referring to the great historical authors
of Greece and Rome, can ever have written with greater

reverence of another than Gibbon of Robertson. He was content, he said, to be the Lepidus in a triumvirate with Robertson and Hume. 'The perfect composition, the nervous language, the well-turned periods of Robertson inflamed me to the ambitious hope that I might one day tread in his footsteps.'[1] In the preface to the fourth volume of the *Decline and Fall* he styled him a 'master-artist'.

It would be difficult to imagine a life fuller, more successful and happier than Robertson's. Born in 1721, a son of the manse, he went to Edinburgh University, was licensed to preach by the Presbytery of Dalkeith when he was twenty, and two years later was presented to a living in East Lothian. He was to style himself a 'moderate Whig', but as a young man he was fervent enough politically to enlist in the first or College Company of Volunteers for the defence of Edinburgh in the '45. As a military detachment they were not impressive. David Hume was to write of them,

> A Friend of mine, who has a poetical genius has made a Description of their march. . . . He compares it to the Course of the *Rhine*, which rolling pompously its Waves through fertile Fields, instead of augmenting in its Course, is continually drawn off by a thousand Canals, and, at last, becomes a small Rivulet, which loses itself in the Land before it reaches the Ocean.[2]

When Edinburgh surrendered without a shot being fired after the rout of the Dragoons at Coltbridge, Robertson offered his services to the English commander, Sir John Cope, but they were declined. However, the historian of the Battle of Pavia had a little more military experience than the Captain of the Hampshire grenadiers. In 1751 he married and he became the

---

[1] *The Autobiography of Edward Gibbon*, ed. John Murray (1896), 167.

[2] [David Hume], *A True Account of the Behaviour and Conduct of Archibald Stewart, Esq.* Quoted in E. C. Mossner, *The Life of David Hume* (1954), 184. (There are references to Robertson during the '45 in Alexander Carlyle, *Autobiography* (1860), 111–30.)

father of a distinguished and united family.[1] He was born in the full flood of the extraordinary literary renaissance in Edinburgh, and the young minister found himself one of the original members of the Select Society, founded by Allan Ramsay, and the friend of philosophers and poets, men such as David Hume, Adam Smith, Adam Ferguson and John Hume. Between them they made that fusion of the Scottish Presbyterian tradition and the Enlightenment which has claims to be the most remarkable intellectual manifestation of the eighteenth century. There was no more stimulating literary atmosphere than in Edinburgh. It should not be forgotten that Robertson's historical work was made possible only by the Advocates' Library. There he found the books which Gibbon was to buy for his own library. The minister of Gladsmuir, a living worth £100 a year, could work with the tools which nearly all his competitors could afford to buy for themselves. There were few other cities in Europe, and, before 1759, none in the British Isles, where that would have been possible.

In 1758 he visited London with Alexander Carlyle and made the acquaintance of Thomas Birch, who arranged for him to study the books which next year were to be available to the public as the British Museum Library. He met Horace Walpole and Smollett; he visited David Garrick at Hampton and watched him play golf. The two Scotsmen returned by Birmingham, where they met Baskerville, and 'through a middle road by Lichfield and Burton-on-Trent, where we could get no drinkable ale, though we threw ourselves there on purpose'.[2] Next year he published his *History of Scotland* and found himself famous. 'I don't know where or what history', wrote Horace Walpole, 'is written with more excellences.'[3] 'There is a

---

[1] 'His wife, though not a woman of parts, was well suited to him, who was more fitted to lead than to be led; and his sons and daughters led so happy a life that his guests, which we were often for a week together, met with nothing but welcome, and peace, and joy.' (Alexander Carlyle, *Autobiography*, 290.)

[2] Alexander Carlyle, *Autobiography*, 372.

[3] *Letters of Horace Walpole*, ed. Mrs Paget Toynbee, IV, 231.

H

history lately come out of the reign of Mary Queen of Scots and King James her son,' wrote Chesterfield to his son, 'written by one Robertson a Scotsman, which for clearness, purity and dignity of style, I will not scruple to compare with the best historians extant, not excepting Davila, Guicciardini, and perhaps Livy.'[1]

Robertson's rise to a leading position in Scotland seems at first sight to be extraordinarily rapid; but when one studies his life one realises that this was not due to his writing a single remarkable book. Quite apart from his histories, one is left with the impression of a man of great weight and soundness of judgment. In 1761 he became Minister of the Old Greyfriars in Edinburgh. As early as 1752, when he was only just over thirty, he had begun to make his mark in the General Assembly of the Church of Scotland. In 1763, in the same year that he was appointed Historiographer to his Majesty in Scotland, he was elected Moderator and for the next sixteen years he completely dominated the Assembly. From 1762 to 1792 he was Principal of Edinburgh University and it is reported that 'during the whole period there did not occur a single question which was not terminated by an unanimous decision'. His biographer, Dugald Stewart, comments — and I think the claim may be accepted — that this 'is perhaps without a parallel in the annals of any other literary community'.[2] He found time to go on writing history, *Charles V* being published in 1769, his *History of America* in 1777, and an *Historical Disquisition concerning the Knowledge which the Ancients had of India; and the Progress of Trade with that country prior to the discovery of the Passage to it by the Cape of Good Hope* in 1791. We have a picture of him in his old age in Henry Cockburn's *Memorials of his Time*,

> He was a pleasant-looking old man; with an eye of great vivacity and intelligence, a large projecting chin, a small hearing trumpet fastened by a black ribbon to a buttonhole

[1] *Letters of Lord Chesterfield*, ed. J. Bradshaw (1913), III, 1254.

[2] D. Stewart, *An Account of the Life and Writings of William Robertson* in W. Robertson, *Works* (1840), I, lxxxiii.

of his coat, and a rather large wig powdered and curled. He struck us boys, even from the side-table, as being evidently fond of a good dinner; at which he sat, with his chin near his plate, intent upon the real business of the occasion. This appearance, however, must have been produced partly by his deafness; because, when his eye told him that there was something interesting, it was delightful to observe the animation with which he instantly applied the trumpet, when, having caught the scent, he followed it up, and was the leader of the pack.[1]

Could any description be imagined more satisfactory and expected? Everything about Robertson was satisfactory and expected.

It may seem surprising, then, to find that Thomas Carlyle wrote to Jane Welsh in 1824 that 'he was a kind of Deist in the guise of a Calvinistic Priest; a portentous combination!'.[2] It was a monstrous exaggeration but in its way an acute judgement. A 'Calvinistic Priest' seems a contradiction in terms. But Robertson's greatest work in the General Assembly was to support the rights of the lay patrons in presenting to livings against the rights of the presbyteries. The answer came fifty years after his death with the secession of the Free Church of Scotland. He was certainly not a deist, but a remarkably calm breeze of toleration breathes through the books in which he dealt with the stormiest period of religious disputes. Writing of the Peace of Augsburg in 1555, he says,

> In our age and nation, to which the idea of Toleration is familiar, and its beneficial effects well known, it may seem strange, that a method of terminating their dissentions, so suitable to the mild and charitable spirit of the Christian religion, did not sooner occur to the contending parties.

He excuses the Protestants by pointing out that their intolerance was really due to the tradition established during the long and dark years of Papal supremacy, and he concludes resignedly,

[1] Henry Cockburn, *Memorials of his Time* (1910), 43–4.
[2] *The Love Letters of Thomas Carlyle and Jane Welsh*, I, 338.

It was towards the close of the seventeenth century, before
Toleration, under its present form, was admitted first into
the republick of the United Provinces, and from thence
introduced into England. Long experience of the calamities
flowing from mutual persecution, the influence of free government, the light and humanity acquired by the progress of
science, together with the prudence and humanity of the
civil magistrate, were all requisite in order to establish a
regulation, so repugnant to the ideas which the different
sects had adopted, from mistaken conceptions concerning
the nature of religion and the rights of truth, or which all
of them had derived from the erroneous maxims established
by the Church of Rome.[1]

He meant what he said. He championed before the General
Assembly his friends David Hume and John Hume, the minister
who had the temerity to write a successful play, *The Tragedy
of Douglas*; he supported Gibbon in the great controversy
which broke out over his Fifteenth and Sixteenth Chapters; in
1779 he spoke in favour of a government bill for removing some
of the disabilities of the Roman Catholics and his house was
attacked by a Protestant mob. But one may wonder whether
such detachment would help any historian to understand the
period of the Reformation. One of the most remarkable
passages in his *Charles V* is a long study of the Jesuit Order and
its influence on European civilisation. Much of it reflects the
hostility to the Order felt in any Protestant country, and, for
that matter, in most Catholic countries, in the eighteenth
century, but it contains also an appreciation of the benefits
derived from it which is unparalleled in protestant literature of
his time. He has nothing but scorn, however, for Ignatius
Loyola, 'a fanatick distinguished by extravagancies in sentiment and conduct, no less incompatible with the maxims of
sober reason, than repugnant to the spirit of true religion'.[2]
And, while he agrees that among the Jesuits have been found

[1] W. Robertson, *The History of the Reign of Charles V* (1769), III,
333–7.
[2] *Charles V*, II, 445.

'eminent mathematicians, antiquarians, and critics', he does not allow them to have 'produced one man, whose mind was so much enlightened with sound knowledge, as to merit the name of a philosopher'. The reason, he decides, is the 'unavoidable effect of monastick education to contract and fetter the human mind'. He concludes with the observation that

> Father Paul of Venice is, perhaps, the only person educated in a cloister, that ever was altogether superior to its pre-judices, or who viewed the transactions of men, and reasoned concerning the interests of society, with the enlarged sentiments of a philosopher, with the discernment of a man conversant in affairs, and with the liberality of a gentleman.[1]

Never did the eighteenth century pronounce more magis-terially upon the past. But if such an attitude would seem to make it difficult to understand the sixteenth century, what would it do if the writer assayed also a study of the Middle Ages? And this is what Robertson did. His *History of the Reign of the Emperor Charles V* is prefaced by a long introduction, more than a quarter of the whole work, entitled, *A View of the Progress of Society in Europe, from the Subversion of the Roman Empire to the Beginning of the Sixteenth Century.* Impressive as the History is as a whole, this introduction is the really important part of it. It was revolutionary and its influence has been profound on all later historical writing.

It is divided into three Sections, the first entitled 'View of the Progress of Society in Europe, with respect to interior Govern-ment, Laws, and Manners'; the second, 'View of the Progress of Society in Europe, with respect to the command of the national force requisite in foreign operations'; and the third, 'View of the political Constitution of the principal States in Europe, at the Commencement of the sixteenth century'. It is in no sense a narrative or chronological account, but rather a series of magnificent generalisations, an attempt to discover the essential movements in society and culture during a thousand years of history. The opening words are themselves a superb

[1] *Charles V*, II, 456.

generalisation, 'Two great revolutions have happened in the political state, and in the manners of the European nations. The first was occasioned by the progress of the Roman power; the second by the subversion of the Roman Empire.'

Robertson owed much to two great writers, Montesquieu and Voltaire, and he handsomely acknowledged the debt. Montesquieu with his broad comparative study of political constitutions and his theories of influences, such as that of climate, on the development of human societies, had led men to try to explain historical events and, although not primarily an historian, in his *Grandeur et Décadence des Romains* he had made a bold effort, on wholly inadequate materials, to put his theories into practice. Voltaire in his *Essai sur les Mœurs* had attempted to do much the same as Robertson, that is to consider the underlying causes of the development of Europe through the Middle Ages. But it is an infuriating book, witty, stimulating, often unexpectedly generous, but wildly incoherent. No wonder the Abbé de Mably said that reading it was as boring as travelling from one town to another without the least idea where one was going.[1]

Robertson, then, was not the first to attempt to discover the essential factors underlying the chronological succession of events in an historical development. The idea was in the air. Even Bolingbroke's rigidly utilitarian demands of History presupposed an attempt to interpret events. And behind all the philosophisings of the eighteenth-century historians were to be heard ancestral voices,

> What were the grounds of quarrel I will first set forth, that in time to come no man may be at a loss to know what was the origin of this great war. The real though unavowed cause I believe to have been the growth of the Athenian power, which terrified the Lacedaemonians and forced them into war; but the reasons publicly alleged on either side were as follows.

But no one before Robertson had made a deliberate, carefully

[1] Quoted in J. B. Black, *The Art of History* (1926), 75.

reasoned and undeviating attempt to show in a series of broad generalisations what were the movements and changes in society which were the underlying causes of events during a long period of history. Anyone who reads now those opening words of Robertson's *History* feels himself at home. That is the way that we think and write about History.

He allowed himself no digressions. One by one he makes his points, explaining the development of feudalism out of the chaos left at the dissolution of the Roman Empire and its effects on society, and then considering in turn the causes of the gradual recovery of Europe from what he calls 'the period of greatest obscuration', the Crusades, 'their influence upon the state of property, and consequently of power' (we constantly meet such phrases, which startle us with their twentieth-century tones); 'the commercial effects of the Crusades'; then 'the forming of cities into communities, corporations or bodies politick' ('if the nobility', he tells us, 'suffered some diminution of their credit and power by the privileges granted to the cities, the crown acquired an increase of both'); to the introduction of 'a more regular, equal, and vigorous administration of justice'; the influence of canon law, 'the revival of the knowledge and study of the Roman law', 'the spirit of Chivalry', 'the progress of science, and the cultivation of literature', and 'the progress of commerce', first in the Italian cities, then in 'the Hanseatick league'. Compared with all this Voltaire's entertaining essay seems very frivolous.

Robertson's *View of the Progress of Society* was to receive a series of devastating salvoes from a great book, Samuel Maitland's *The Dark Ages*, first published in 1839. Robertson's general attitude towards the Middle Ages was conventional and inevitable in his age, the same as that of Voltaire, Hume and Gibbon. Maitland was able to convict him of errors of scholarship in interpreting his sources, which were obviously the result of prejudice. His most serious charge — and he proves it to the hilt — was that Robertson generalised far too freely from isolated incidents. Evidence of illiteracy or barbaric customs in one part of Europe is taken as being applicable to some quite different part and, what was an even more serious failing, evidence from one century as applicable to centuries later. (Perhaps we should not be too hard on him to-day. Anyone who reads historical text-books finds exactly the same misuse of evidence in, for example, their descriptions of French society before the Revolution.) Robertson did not know enough to write on so immense a theme. For all that, he knew a great deal. His introduction was made possible only by the work of the antiquaries of the previous hundred years, the Benedictine scholars, Muratori, Du Cange, Bouquet and others, and by the publication of the great chronicles of the Middle Ages, the Byzantine historians and the Western chroniclers from Gregory of Tours to Philippe de Commines. The use he made of them was, again, original. No one before him had grounded his generalisations so firmly on the texts he used for his sources or had taken such trouble to show what he was doing. One half of his introduction consists of what he called 'Proofs and Illustrations', printed at the end of the volume, forty-four notes, some of them considerable essays. He seemed to be almost ashamed of them, but it was in a paragraph in his Preface excusing them that he wrote in a way which speaks directly to the future. Here for the first time we find that union of generalisation and research on which modern historical writing is based. 'In this part of my work', he begins, 'I have been led into several critical disquisitions, which belong more properly to the province of the lawyer or antiquary, than to that of the historian,' but, he concludes,

> As my inquiries conducted me often into paths which were obscure or little frequented, such constant recourse to the authors who have been my guides, was not only necessary for authenticating the facts which are the foundations of my reasonings, but may be useful in pointing out the way to such as shall hereafter hold the same course, and in enabling them to carry on their researches with greater facility and success.[1]

[1] *Charles V*, I, xii–xiii.

He did not really believe that the province of the lawyer was a different one from that of the historian. In the last sentence of his final note he makes a statement, prophetic of the kind of history which was to be written during the next two hundred years.

> While engaged in perusing the laws, charters, and early historians of the continental kingdoms, I have often been led to think that an attempt to illustrate the progress of the English jurisprudence and policy, by a comparison with those of other kingdoms in a similar situation, would be of great utility, and might throw much light on some points which are now obscure, and decide others, which have long been contraverted.[1]

When Robertson turned to the main theme of his book, however, that which is covered by its title, he kept very closely to what he considered to be 'the province of the historian'. It is, in the strictest sense, political history. His main interest lay in the external relationships of the states of Western Europe, their negotiations, alliances and wars. The period of which he was writing was dominated by a great revolution, the Protestant Reformation, but he dealt much more thoroughly with its political effects in Germany than with the Reformation itself. Writing to Horace Walpole about his intention to write on the reign of Charles V he explained that 'the events are great and interesting . . . the rivalship between Charles and Francis; their intrigues with Henry VIII are splendid objects in history. The inferior characters too are good . . . [they] are pleasant or (which is as lucky for an historian) strange figures'. It is astonishing to find that the future Moderator should include Luther among the 'inferior characters', along with Leo X, the Constable Bourbon and the Marquis de Pescara.[2] He made no attempt to analyse the religious ideas of Luther; he never once mentioned, for instance, the doctrine of Justification by Faith. He touched

[1] *Charles V*, I, 394.
[2] Horace Walpole's Correspondence, ed. W. S. Lewis, Yale Edition (1952), XV, 46.

on the relationship between Luther and Erasmus, but went no
more deeply into it than to say that Erasmus 'first scattered
the seeds, which Luther cherished and brought to maturity'
and to decide that it was 'the natural timidity of his temper'
which 'prevented Erasmus from holding the same course with
Luther'.[1] There is nothing on the great debate between them
on Free Will and Election, a controversy of decisive importance
in religious history. He neglected completely the disputes
between the Lutherans and Zwinglians. He never even mentioned Calvin. He could not avoid some attempt to explain the
circumstances which made possible the sudden and widespread
acceptance of Luther's opinions, but he felt it somewhat
irrelevant to his task.

> It is evident, that their success was the natural effect of
> many powerful causes prepared by peculiar providence, and
> happily conspiring to that end. This attempt to investigate
> these causes, and to throw light on an event so singular and
> important, will not, perhaps, be deemed an unnecessary
> digression. — I return from it to the course of the history.[2]

'The course of the history', though the phrase is thus
narrowly interpreted, was managed in a masterly way. He had
an exceedingly complicated story to tell, the struggle between
the Valois and the Hapsburg, the rising of the Communeros in
Spain and the settlement in that country, the intricate diplomatic relationships of the Italian states, the political effects of
the Reformation in Germany, the slow progress of the Roman
Church towards the Council of Trent, the conquests of Charles
V in North Africa, which obviously interested him a great deal,
and the attacks of the Ottoman Turks. (He reserved the conquests of Spain in the New World for a later book.) He kept
strictly to a chronological scheme. It was necessary for him to
be in continual motion over the whole European arena. He had
his narrative under complete control; he managed his changes
of scene with the utmost dexterity. His skill in handling his
material, keeping all the various fields he has to cover under a

[1] *Charles V*, II, 119.   [2] *Charles V*, II, 120–1.

constant survey, cannot be illustrated by quotations; it is
fascinating to see how he does it. He moves from Spain to Italy,
then to a general consideration of European diplomatic relationships, from this to a study of the internal difficulties of Francis
I, to Germany and the growing power of the princes, to a year's
campaigns of Solyman the Magnificent, without once seeming
to break the thread of the narrative. One is left with nothing
but admiration for his competence.

Robertson was capable of telling a good incidental story,
such as the account in his *History of Scotland* of the murder of
Rizzio, or in his *History of America* of the landfall of Columbus.
In neither case does one have the impression that he felt that
anything special was demanded of him. They are clear and
accurate, but not very vivid. In his *Charles V*, however, he
denied himself any stories at all, and this must have been
deliberate. There were incidents enough over which he might
have allowed himself to linger for a few moments, the Diet of
Worms, the Sack of Rome, the siege of Vienna, the meeting
between Luther and the Zwinglians at Marburg, which he
never even mentioned, the flight of the Emperor from Inns-
bruck; but he rejected almost every opportunity. The only
occasion when we feel that the interest of the story allowed him
to dwell on an incident was when he described the love of
Solyman the Magnificent for Roxelana and the murder of his
son, Mustapha.

One might argue, somewhat austerely, that Robertson was
justified, that he had set out to give a lucid, well-proportioned
and convincing survey, and that to linger over certain episodes
would have destroyed its clarity and balance. But this does not
make for stimulating writing. It is a more serious charge that
he had no feeling for the relevant and illuminating detail. One
example out of hundreds may be taken from Gibbon of the way
in which detail may help an historian. He is writing of a critical
moment in the history of the Byzantine Empire, the successful
diplomacy of the Emperor Alexius Comnenus in gaining some
control over the warriors of the First Crusade, especially over
his old enemy, the Norman Bohemond from South Italy.

The hateful Bohemond was received as a true and ancient ally; and, if the emperor reminded him of former hostilities, it was only to praise the valour that he had displayed, and the glory that he had acquired, in the fields of Durazzo and Larissa. The son of Guiscard was lodged and entertained, and served with Imperial pomp: one day, as he passed through the gallery of the palace, a door was carelessly left open to expose a pile of gold and silver, of silk and gems, of curious and costly furniture, that was heaped in seeming disorder from the floor to the roof of the chamber. 'What conquests', exclaimed the ambitious miser, 'might not be achieved by the possession of such a treasure!' 'It is your own,' replied a Greek attendant, who watched the motions of his soul; and Bohemond, after some hesitation, condescended to accept this magnificent present. The Norman was flattered by the assurance of an independent principality; and Alexius eluded, rather than denied, his daring demand of the office of great domestic, or general of the East.[1]

Read the passage without the little story of the pile of treasure and one has all that is required for the point Gibbon wanted to make, that Alexius diplomatically secured some control over his dangerous ally. But the story, used with Gibbon's skill, enabled him to emphasise certain aspects which were most relevant to his purpose, the contrast between the wealth of Constantinople and the primitive standards of Crusaders, the cunning of the Byzantine diplomacy, the naivety of the Western soldier. Such passages stand up to — and indeed repay — the most exacting analysis. 'That was heaped in *seeming* disorder.' One realises how neatly one has just been led up a little side-path in the garden, with the words 'a door was *carelessly* left open'. But there is more to it than that. When you read of the door carelessly left open you are Bohemond, taken in as he was; when you read of the seeming disorder, you are Alexius Comnenus, who had arranged that open door.

[1] E. Gibbon, *The History of the Decline and Fall of the Roman Empire*, ed. J. B. Bury (1912), VI, 300–1.

We shall find nothing like this in Robertson's history. It might be thought that the lack of relevant detail was due to the fact that Robertson never acquired it. He admitted with complacency that he was unable to read books written in the German language. But actually those works which he was able to consult gave him enough details to enliven his history, if he had cared to use them. Robertson did not want to use them. When introducing Rizzio into his *History of Scotland*, he had written, 'The low birth and indigent condition of this man placed him in a station in which he ought naturally to have remained unknown to posterity. But what fortune called him to act and suffer in Scotland, obliges history to descend from its dignity, and to record his adventures.' The 'dignity of history' (the phrase was Bolingbroke's[1]) not only made it distasteful to write about one who 'was the son of a musician in Turin, and, having accompanied the Piedmontese Ambassador into Scotland, gained admission into the Queen's family by his skill in music'.[2] It also put him continually on his guard against descending to the trivial. In the whole *History of the Reign of Charles V* he allowed himself to quote only ten remarks which were not public pronouncements.[3] Of all Johnson's strange, wrong-headed judgements, there can be few to equal his criticism of Robertson that he 'detains you a great deal too long. No man will read Robertson's cumbrous detail a second time'.[4]

An interesting study might be made of the verdicts delivered by eighteenth-century authors on one another's style. It is difficult to find any common standard among them. Gibbon, we may remember, spoke of Robertson's 'perfect composition, nervous language and well-turned periods'. 'Let me hear no

[1] *Letters on the Study and Use of History*, Letter V. 'Read Thucydides or Xenophon . . . they maintained the dignity of history, and thought it beneath them to vamp up old traditions, like the writers of their age and country, and to be the trumpeters of a lying antiquity.'

[2] W. Robertson, *History of Scotland*, Sixth Edition (1771), I, 275.

[3] He permitted himself, however, one unique, almost Gibbonian footnote, describing the wrestling-match between Francis I and Henry VIII at the Field of the Cloth of Gold.

[4] *Boswell's Life of Johnson*, II, 237.

more of the tinsel of Robertson,' exclaimed Johnson — but he
was talking to a Scotsman.[1] 'Robertson', he said, 'used pretty
words' — and this time he was talking to an Irishman.[2] These
judgements are worthless. But Johnson's main criticism of
Robertson was of his 'verbiage'.[3] He had 'too many words, and
those too big ones'.[4] 'Robertson', he declared to Boswell, 'is
like a man who has packed gold in wool: the wool takes up
more room than the gold. No, Sir; I always thought Robertson
would be crushed by his own weight — would be buried under
his own ornaments.'[5] Johnson was hardly the one to make
these comments. Robertson himself once claimed to have
deduced that Johnson was the author of an anonymous work,
The Memoirs of Frederick III, King of Prussia, from one
sentence in it, describing Frederick William's delight in his
regiment of the tallest soldiers in Europe. 'To review this
towering regiment was his daily pleasure, and to perpetuate it
was so much his care, that when he met a tall woman he
immediately commanded one of his *Titanian* retinue to marry
her, that they might *propagate procerity*.' That was just how
Robertson did not write.[6]

Let me take two passages which are reasonably typical of his
style.

The court of Rome beheld this growing defection with great
concern; and Adrian's first care after his arrival in Italy, had
been to deliberate with the Cardinals, concerning the proper
means of putting a stop to it. This Pope was profoundly
skilled in scholastic theology, and having been early taken
notice of on that account, he still retained such an excessive
admiration of the science to which he owed his reputation
and success in life, that he considered Luther's invectives
against the schoolmen, particularly Thomas Aquinas, as
little less than blasphemy. All the tenets of that doctor
appeared to him so clear and irrefragable, that he supposed
every person who called in question or contradicted them, to

[1] *Johnsonian Miscellanies*, ed. G. B. Hill (1897), II, 10.

[2] *Ibid.*, II, 48.   [3] *Boswell's Life of Johnson*, II, 236.

[4] *Ibid.*, III, 173.   [5] *Ibid.*, II, 237.   [6] *Ibid.*, I, 308.

be either blinded by ignorance, or to be acting in opposition
to the conviction of his own mind: Of course, no Pope was
ever more bigoted or inflexible with regard to points of
doctrine than Adrian; he not only maintained them as Leo
had done, because they were ancient, or because it was
dangerous for the church to allow of innovations, but he
adhered to them with the zeal of a theologian, and with
tenaciousness of a disputant.[1]

Here is an example of his narrative style.

Vast arrears were due to his troops, whom he had long
amused with vain hopes and promises. As they now foresaw
that little attention would be paid to their demands, when
by the re-establishment of peace their services became of less
importance, they lost all patience, broke out into open
mutiny, and declared that they thought themselves entitled
to seize by violence what was detained from them contrary to
all justice. Nor was this spirit of sedition confined to one part
of the Emperor's dominions; the mutiny was almost as general as the grievance which gave rise to it. The soldiers in the
Milanese plundered the open country without controul, and
filled the capital itself with consternation. Those in garrison
at Goletta threatened to give up that important fortress to
Barbarossa. In Sicily the troops proceeded to still greater
excesses; having chaced away their officers, they elected
others in their stead, defeated a body of men whom the
viceroy sent against them, took and pillaged several cities,
conducting themselves all the while, in such a manner, that
their operations resembled rather the regular proceedings of
a concerted rebellion, than the rashness and violence of a
military mutiny.[2]

It was absurd to speak of Robertson's style as 'verbiage', but
we must remember that Boswell was a Scotsman and that
Johnson probably criticised Robertson to him so continually
because he knew that Boswell would always rise to the fly.
At any rate, he never disclosed to Boswell that the printer
of *Charles V* had sent him the manuscript to correct. Nor is

[1] *Charles V*, II, 206–7.   [2] *Charles V*, II, 427–8.

there any reason to suppose that Robertson was aware of it.[1]

It would be difficult to imagine a more efficient or a clearer style than Robertson's. There is not a sentence in the *Charles V* of which the meaning is not perfectly plain, and, although it gives an impression of sonority, there is rarely an unnecessary word. The sentences are balanced and rhythmical; it is possible to see why they were admired by Gibbon. A shrewder criticism than Johnson's was levelled against his style by two who both admired it, Lord Mansfield and Edmund Burke. Mansfield said that although he could point out few or no faults in his books, yet when he was reading them, 'he did not think he was reading English.'[2] Burke praised Robertson's style, but said, 'he writes like a man who composes in a dead language which he understands but cannot speak.'[3] Boswell once carried out a curious experiment. He claimed to have invented a kind of shorthand or rather note-taking of his own, which enabled him to take down 'the substance and language of any discourse' which he had heard. (We owe to it his *Life of Johnson*.) Johnson refused to believe him and read him 'slowly and distinctly' a passage from Robertson's *History of America*. 'It was found that I had it very imperfectly; the conclusion from which was, that its excellence was principally owing to a studied arrangement of words, which could not be varied or abridged without an essential injury.'[4]

[1] *Letters of Samuel Johnson*, ed. G. B. Hill (1892), I, 499. Johnson, writing to Strahan, the printer, refers to Robert Watson's *History of the Reign of Philip II* and asks if he can 'give any help, or be of any use, as formerly in Dr Robertson's publication'. The letter is dated 14 October 1776. Strahan had been one of the publishers of Robertson's *History of Scotland* in 1759, but Johnson is probably referring to his more recent publication of *Charles V* in 1769.

[2] Alexander Carlyle, *Autobiography*, 57. (Mansfield thought the same of David Hume.)

[3] M. Forbes, *Beattie and his Friends* (1904), quoted in *Boswell's Life of Johnson*, I, 549. (It may be pointed out as corroborative evidence that Robertson is a favourite author of those who set passages for translation into Latin prose.)

[4] *Boswell's Life of Johnson*, III, 270.

'A studied arrangement of words' describes Robertson's
style very well. It is lucid and most efficiently controlled; it
cannot be called laboured; but it is altogether lacking in
spontaneity. Its dignity is maintained for hundreds of pages,
but one comes to long for some relief. Robertson was too
conscious of his duties as a judge of men's actions in the past
to allow himself more than very occasionally even the relief of
irony, which was the means by which Gibbon relieved continually a style as carefully constructed as Robertson's. When
Robertson does allow himself to be ironic it is usually at the
expense of the Roman Church. Writing of the election of Pope
Adrian VI,

> The Cardinals themselves, unable to give a reason for this
> strange choice, on account of which, as they marched in pro-
> cession from the conclave, they were loaded with insults and
> curses by the Roman people, ascribed it to an immediate
> impulse of the Holy Ghost. It may be imputed with greater
> certainty to the influence of Don John Manuel, the Imperial
> ambassador, who by his address and intrigues facilitated the
> election of a person devoted to his master's service, from
> gratitude, from interest, and from inclination.[1]

Writing of the historians of the Council of Trent,

> But whichsoever of these authors an intelligent person takes
> for a guide, in forming a judgment concerning the spirit of
> the council, he must discover so much ambition as well as
> artifice among some of the members, so much ignorance and
> corruption among others; he must observe such a large
> infusion of human policy and passions, but such a scanty
> portion of that simplicity of heart, sanctity of manners, and
> love of truth, which alone qualify men to determine what
> doctrines are worthy of God, and what worship is accept-
> able to him; that he will find it no easy matter to believe,
> that any extraordinary influence of the Holy Ghost hovered
> over this assembly, and dictated its decrees.[2]

One passage echoes the other, but there is half the work between

[1] *Charles V*, II, 146.   [2] *Ibid.*, III, 248.

I

them and from one to the other he hardly ever allows himself anything like the little fling which he indulged in here with the word 'extraordinary'. Nor was Robertson capable of producing the epigrammatic sentences with which Gibbon was able to sum up his conclusions. 'The various modes of worship, which prevailed in the Roman world, were all considered by the people as equally true; by the philosopher, as equally false; and by the magistrate, as equally useful.'[1] Robertson could generalise, but he could never express his generalities like that.

There were some at the time of its publication who were not ready to praise the book. John Wesley, whose literary judgments are of little value, said of the first volume with the Introduction, 'I know not when I have been so disappointed. Here is a quarto volume of eight or ten shillings' price, containing dry, verbose dissertations on feudal government, the substance of all which might be comprised in half a sheet of paper.'[2] Horace Walpole, who had been loud in his praises of the *History of Scotland*, seems to have positively disliked the *Charles V*, though he never disclosed his reasons. It was not, as one might imagine, that he reacted against Robertson's failure to appreciate the Middle Ages, for he spoke of the Introduction, when it was first published, with some approval.[3] But, apart from a few critics, the book was an immense success. It was the work which made Robertson famous in Europe. Voltaire, on the receipt of a copy, wrote in homage, 'You are eloquent, learned and impartial. I join with Europe in expressing my esteem.'[4] The Empress Catherine the Great said that she took it with her on all her journeys: 'I never leave off reading it, particularly the first volume.' Her appreciation of it was a very shrewd one and she showed that she understood the real originality of Robertson, that his history was more than narrative, but a continuous judicial effort to explain the

[1] *Decline and Fall of the Roman Empire*, I, 31.

[2] John Wesley, *Journal* (April 28, 1772).

[3] *Letters of Horace Walpole*, ed. Mrs Paget Toynbee, X, 60 (10 June, 1777), 226 (April 1778).

[4] D. Stewart, *op. cit.*, I, xxxvii.

course of events. What she admired, she said, was 'that sagacity
and discernment displayed by you in painting the human mind
and character, as diversified by the various causes that operated
upon it'.[1]

The modern student of the development of historical writing,
like Mr Edmund Wilson in his *To the Finland Station*, will probably trace the genesis of the historical attitude of to-day
through Michelet back to Vico. Vico, whose *Scienza Nuova*
appeared when Robertson was four years old, was a lone
genius, one of those fated to wait until rediscovered in an age
better able to understand him. There is no reason to think that
Robertson had ever heard of him. Robertson was no philosopher. Vico with his statements of the general principles of
historical study could stimulate a writer, such as Michelet,
in a way that Robertson could never have done. But in his
Introduction, writing as an historian and without fully
realising where his inquiries were leading him, Robertson often
took up a position which shows that the minds of the two
writers, though working in very different ways, were moving in
the same direction. 'The nature of things', wrote Vico, 'is
nothing other than that they come into being at certain times
and in certain ways. Wherever the same circumstances are
present, the same phenomena arise and no other.' After discussing at length the information to be found in Caesar and
Tacitus 'concerning the ancient state of the barbarous nations',
Robertson added,

> Before I quit this subject, it may not be improper to observe,
> that though successive alterations in their institutions, to-
> gether with the gradual progress of refinement, have made an
> entire change in the manners of the various people, who
> conquered the Roman Empire, there is still one race of men
> nearly in the same political situation with that in which they
> were when they first settled in their new conquests: I mean
> the various tribes and nations of Savages in North America.
> It cannot then be considered either as a digression, or as an
> improper indulgence of curiosity to enquire, whether this

[1] D. Stewart, *op. cit.*, I, cxv.

similarity in their political state has occasioned any resemblance between their character and manners. If the likeness turns out to be striking, it is a stronger proof that a just account has been given of the ancient inhabitants of Europe, than the testimony even of Caesar or of Tacitus.[1]

That Robertson's study of 'the Savages of North America', which was derived from only one book, Charlevoix's *Journal Historique d'un Voyage de l'Amérique*, is utterly superficial, need not concern us here. What matters is that he discovered, one might almost say stumbled on, an entirely new line of historical inquiry. His conclusion is very remarkable.

It is sufficient for my purpose to have pointed out the similarity of those great features which distinguish and and characterize both people. Bochart, and other philologists of the last century, who, with more erudition than science, endeavoured to trace the migrations of various nations, and who were apt, upon the slightest appearance of resemblance, to find an affinity between nations far removed from each other, and to conclude that they were descended from the same ancestors, would hardly have failed, on viewing such an amazing similarity, to pronounce with confidence, 'That the Germans and Americans must be the same people.' But a philosopher will satisfy himself with observing, 'That the characters of nations depend on the state of society in which they live, and on the political institutions established among them; and that the human mind, whenever it is placed in the same situation, will, in ages the most distant, and in countries the most remote, assume the same form, and be distinguished by the same manners.'[2]

Vico would have gone further. He would have held that the political institutions also would have depended on the state of the society. The difference is profoundly important. But Robertson showed on several occasions that he was, in fact, aware that political institutions depended on changes in the structure of society. In the course of a long note on 'the

[1] *Charles V*, I, 209.   [2] *Charles V*, I, 211.

history of the establishment and progress of the feudal system',
he says,

> This revolution in property occasioned a change correspond-
> ing to it in political government; the great vassals of the
> crown, as they acquired such extensive possessions, usurped
> a proportional degree of power, depressed the jurisdiction of
> the crown, and trampled on the privileges of the people. It
> is on account of this connection, that the tracing of the
> progress of feudal property becomes an object of attention in
> history; for upon discovering in what state property was at
> any particular period, we may determine with precision what
> was the degree of power possessed by the King or the
> nobility at that juncture.[1]

Robertson's tendency to produce generalisations, or
'theories', as they were called, used to amuse his friends.
Alexander Carlyle once told a story of his being in England
with three companions, Dundas, Cockburn and Sinclair. The
three,

> seeing a gallows on a neighbouring hillock, rode round to
> have a nearer view of the felon on the gallows. When they
> met in the inn, Robertson immediately began a dissertation
> on the character of nations, and how much the English, like
> the Romans, were hardened by their cruel diversions of cock-
> fighting, bull-baiting, bruising, &c.; for had they not
> observed three Englishmen on horse-back do what no
> Scotchman or — . Here Dundas, having compassion,
> interrupted him, and said, 'What! did you not know,
> Principal, that it was Cockburn and Sinclair and me?' This
> put an end to theories &c. for that day.[2]

The story is illuminating. One can see Robertson's mind at
work. Few men before him had thought in this way; none had,
perhaps, been so constantly eager to discover the underlying
causes of the character of nations or of historical developments.
In this lay his strength and his originality. But it must be
admitted that his 'theories' were often as insecurely grounded

[1] *Charles V*, I, 222.   [2] Alexander Carlyle, *Autobiography*, 286–7.

as those which sprang into his mind as he watched the three riders approach the gallows. That is one reason why he is not read to-day. After Samuel Maitland's devastating criticism no one was likely to expect to find in Robertson's Introduction a true picture of the Middle Ages.

But this was not the only reason why he is now forgotten. He lacked visual imagination. He seems to have taken several years to decide that the Reign of Charles V was to be the subject of his next work after the History of Scotland. One cannot imagine the idea starting into his mind, as it did with Gibbon, inspired by sights and sounds. There are, it is true, a few occasions when one feels that he has in his mind a picture of what he is writing about. To give Robertson his due it was one of these, the account of Balboa reaching the Pacific, which inspired Keats, whose memory for names was faulty, to write of Cortez, 'silent upon a peak in Darien'. But even here the ordinary reader is not likely to feel with any unusual vividness that he is there himself.

> As soon as he beheld the South Sea stretching in endless prospect below him, he fell on his knees, and lifting up his hands to Heaven, returned thanks to God, who had conducted him to a discovery so beneficial to his country, and so honourable to himself. His followers, observing his transports of joy, rushed forward to join him in his wonder, exultation and gratitude.[1]

> And all his men
> Look'd at each other with a wild surmise.

It would not be so very surprising to find these actual words in Gibbon. If I had to choose one sentence to show the distance between the two historians, it would be from a footnote in the *Decline and Fall*. Gibbon is describing the preparations for the invasion of Africa by Belisarius.

> From a laudable desire to assert the dignity of his theme, Procopius defends the soldiers of his own time against the morose critics who confined the respectable name to the

---

[1] W. Robertson, *History of America* (1777), I, 204.

heavy-armed warriors of antiquity and maliciously observed that the word archer is introduced by Homer as a term of contempt. 'Such contempt' [here he quotes from Procopius] 'might, perhaps, be due to the naked youths who appeared on foot in the fields of Troy, and, lurking behind a tomb-stone, or the shield of a friend, drew the bow-string to their breast, and dismissed a feeble and lifeless arrow.'

In a footnote he gives the relevant line from the *Iliad* and then he adds,

How concise — how just — how beautiful is the whole pic-ture! I see the attitudes of the archer — I hear the twanging of the bow.[1]

Robertson did not see or hear.

He will not be read, then, but he should not be forgotten. All of us who are interested in history owe more to him than we realise. 'In this epoch of full-grown history', said Acton of the modern world, 'men have not acquiesced in the given condition of their lives. Taking little for granted, they have sought to know the ground they stand on, and the road they travel, and the reason why.'[2] Among the writers who have made us think like that, William Robertson may claim a distinguished place.

[1] *Decline and Fall of the Roman Empire*, IV, 295.
[2] Lord Acton, *Lectures on Modern History* (1921), 5.

V

Thomas Moore
Lalla Rookh

'Mr Moore', said Hazlitt, 'ought not to have written *Lalla Rookh*.'[1] We may agree. But we cannot accept his subsequent judgment that his admirers wanted something quite different. *Lalla Rookh* was at once an immense success. It was continually reissued in this country, and twenty years after its first appearance its publisher referred to it as 'the cream of the copyrights'. It was quickly translated into many foreign languages. Chateaubriand sang its praises;[2] Stendhal said that he had read it five times;[3] and when Goethe told Eckermann that, since he was ignorant of Greek and Latin, he had better learn English, the language of Byron, Moore and Scott, he was thinking of *Lalla Rookh*.[4]

No one reads *Lalla Rookh* now. The most that can be said for Moore's songs and ballads, the *Irish Melodies* and the *National Airs*, some of which are still familiar, is that they are better than most Victorian drawing-room ballads, which derived from them and among which they soon took their place. They have a certain period charm and, as one reads them, one automatically pictures the scene, the dresses of the ladies and the whiskers of the gentlemen, and hears the piano beginning its all too obvious accompaniment. What seems

[1] William Hazlitt, *Lectures on the English Poets*, Lecture VIII.

[2] *Memoirs, Journal and Correspondence of Thomas Moore*, ed. Lord John Russell (1853–6), III, 203.

[3] Moore, *Memoirs*, III, 109.

[4] Johann Peter Eckermann, *Gespräche mit Goethe*, 3 December. 1824.

extraordinary is that poets like Shelley or Landor could have
approved of them so highly.

> Faintly as tolls the evening chime,
> Our voices keep tune and our oars keep time.
> Soon as the woods on shore look dim,
> We'll sing at St. Ann's our parting hymn.
> Row, brothers, row, the stream runs fast,
> The Rapids are near and the day light past.
>
>   *   *   *
>
> Oft in the stilly night,
>   Ere Slumber's chain has bound me,
> Fond Memory brings the Light
>   Of other days around me.
>
>   *   *   *
>
> So warmly we met and so fondly we parted,
>   That which was the sweeter ev'n I could not tell.
>
>   *   *   *
>
> The Minstrel Boy to the war is gone,
>   In the ranks of death you'll find him;
> His father's sword he has girded on,
>   And his wild harp slung behind him.

or, for we had better be aware of all that Moore was capable of,

> When through the Piazetta
>   Night breathes her cool air,
> Then, dearest Ninetta,
>   I'll come to thee there.
> Beneath thy mask shrouded,
>   I'll know thee afar,
> As Love knows, though clouded,
>   His own evening star.

'I am strongly inclined to think', wrote Moore, when he had written almost all his poetry, 'that, in a race into future times (if
anything of mine could pretend to such a run,) those little ponies,
the Melodies, will beat the mare, Lalla, hollow.'[1] All his horses
are out of the race now, but I should not agree with the verdict. If
I had to risk any money, it would be placed on *Lalla Rookh*.

[1] Moore, *Memoirs*, VIII, 277.

But if Moore's poetry is forgotten, he himself is not. His friendship with Byron and the mysterious story of the destruction of Byron's *Memoirs* have been enough to ensure him a place in English literary history. It should not be necessary, therefore, for me to say much about his life, though *Lalla Rookh* is a more personal poem than might be thought at first sight. He was born in Dublin in 1779. His life was a fantastic success-story. The son of a Dublin grocer, he became a leading figure in London society and his *Memoirs* were edited after his death by a Prime Minister, while he was holding the office. He came of a Catholic family who were interested in politics at a highly dangerous time. As a boy he was taken to a dinner given in honour of Napper Tandy and noticed by the great man; he became a close friend of Robert Emmet; he risked his place at Trinity College, Dublin, by stating at an inquiry held there that he refused to answer any question which might incriminate others. But, although I think it must be agreed that his devotion to Ireland was genuine, that was the biggest risk he ever took. He was ill during the 1798 rebellion and next year he began to read for the Bar in London. In 1800, when he was twenty-one years old, he published his first book, a translation of the Odes of Anacreon. His attempt to secure the help of Trinity College was unsuccessful; the Provost 'expressed his doubts whether the Board could properly confer any public reward upon the translation of a work so amatory and convivial as the Odes of Anacreon'. But his luck was with him. He brought it out by subscription; Thomas Campbell agreed to subscribe; then Mrs Fitzherbert; and then the Prince of Wales accepted the dedication. The Prince 'said that he hoped when he returned to town in the winter, we should have many opportunities of enjoying each other's society; that he was passionately fond of music and had long heard of my talents that way'.[1] Moore had found an unusual way into London society; he became known as an amateur singer to his own piano accompaniment, who could draw tears from every eye. The Prince meant what he said when he claimed to be 'pas-

[1] Moore, *Memoirs*, I, 108.

sionately fond of music'. He too liked to sing after dinner, and he and Moore would often share the honours of an evening.

Other volumes of poems followed, *The Poetical Works of Tom Little* in 1801, songs sold in sheets with their music, *Epistles, Odes and other Poems* in 1806, and, between 1808 and 1815, six volumes of *Irish Melodies.* He was always in debt and always escaping from financial disaster. In 1811 he made an utterly improvident marriage with an Irish actress aged seventeen and found himself with the perfect wife. They retired to an idyllic country cottage, 'a little nut-shell of a thing' Moore called it, near Ashbourne in Derbyshire and he settled down to write a poem, the idea for which had been in his mind for some months. 'I shall now take to my poem,' he wrote to a friend, 'and do something, I hope, that will place me above the vulgar herd of worldlings and of critics; but you shall hear from me again, when I get among the maids of Cashmere, the sparkling springs of Rochabad, and the fragrant banquets of the Peris.'[1]

It is difficult to convey the charm of Moore's society, and yet I doubt whether it is possible to understand *Lalla Rookh* without appreciating it. Benjamin Haydon in his *Memoirs* speaks of him,

Met Moore at dinner, and spent a very pleasant three hours. He told his stories with a hit-or-miss air, as if accustomed to people of rapid apprehension. It being asked at Paris who they would have as a godfather for Rothschild's child, 'Talleyrand,' said a Frenchman. 'Pourquoi, Monsieur?' 'Prace qu'il est le moins Chrétien possible.'

It would seem difficult to imagine a much more pointless anecdote, but Haydon continues,

Unless one had heard Moore tell the above story of Talleyrand, it would have been impossible to conceive the air of half-suppressed impudence, the delicate, light-horse canter of phrase with which the words floated out of his sparkling Anacreontic mouth.[2]

[1] Moore, *Memoirs*, VIII, 92–3.
[2] *The Autobiography and Memoirs of Benjamin Robert Haydon* (1926), 350–1, (23 March 1824).

Perhaps the best way to give an impression of Thomas Moore would be to tell the story of a completely absurd incident in his life, his duel with Jeffrey, the editor of the *Edinburgh Review*.[1] It has claims to be the most absurd incident in the history of English literature. Moore had just brought out his *Epistles, Odes and other Poems*, and Jeffrey decided that the young poet should be properly taken to task. The author, he said, was 'the most licentious of modern versifiers and the most poetical of those who in our time have devoted their talents to the propagation of immorality', and he called the book 'a cold-blooded attempt to corrupt the purity of unknown and unsuspecting readers'. Moore decided that his only course was to call Jeffrey out. His first difficulty was that Jeffrey was, he believed, in Edinburgh and he could not afford the fare to Scotland. Then, having learnt that Jeffrey was in London, he had some trouble in finding a second. However, eventually his friend, Dr Thomas Hume, agreed to act and Jeffrey secured the services of Francis Horner. It was settled that they should meet next morning at Chalk Farm, but another difficulty arose. Neither Moore nor Jeffrey owned a pistol and the weapons had to be borrowed by Moore from a friend. When they all arrived at Chalk Farm next morning, it was discovered that Horner, Jeffrey's second, was completely ignorant of firearms and the loading of Jeffrey's pistol had to be entrusted to Moore's second, Hume. By the time the two seconds were ready, the principals were engaged in a friendly conversation. Moore had made a conventional remark about the weather, which was quite enough to set Jeffrey off. However, honour demanded that the duel should proceed; they took up their positions and raised their pistols, when a crowd of police-officers jumped out of the neighbouring bushes and arrested them. The lender of the pistols had dined out on the story and, as a result, a Bow Street magistrate had been informed. As they waited at Bow Street for bail to be arranged, Jeffrey lay at full length on a bench and talked about literature.

So far the incident had been ridiculous enough, but worse

[1] Moore, *Memoirs* I, 199–214.

was to follow. Moore, after he had been released on bail, realised that he had forgotten the pistols. On returning to retrieve them, he found a constable perplexed at the discovery that Moore's pistol had a bullet in it, but Jeffrey's had not. The seconds had been incompetent, but it did not look very well. Moore tried to persuade the seconds to sign an explanation, but Hume decided that he had made a fool enough of himself already. It took Moore a long time to forgive his friend. On top of all that, a newspaper account substituted the word 'pellet' for 'bullet' and the most was made of the misprint, if that is what is was. It was a mistake for Moore to try to save his dignity by writing a letter to *The Times*. But what came out of it all was an enduring friendship between Moore and Jeffrey. Thirty-seven years later Moore wrote in his diary: 'Breakfasted at Rogers's, to meet Jeffrey and Lord John, — two of the men I like best among my numerous friends. Jeffrey's volubility (which was always superabundant) becomes even more copious, I think, as he grows older. But I am ashamed of myself for finding *any* fault with him. Long may he flourish "in omne volubilis ævum".' By a pleasant coincidence the entry continued, 'Walked about a good deal with Hume, or rather cabbed with him; he paying as usual the damage.'[1]

But we have not finished with the after-effects of the duel. In 1809 Byron referred to it in *English Bards and Scotch Reviewers*.

> Can none remember that eventful day,
> That ever-glorious, almost fatal fray,
> When Little's leadless pistol met his eye,
> And Bow-street Myrmidons stood laughing by?

Moore demanded satisfaction, but met with his usual ill-luck in affairs of honour. Byron was abroad and never received the challenge. When he returned, nearly two years later, Moore found it rather difficult to keep up the pressure. However, he insisted that the insult should be 'retracted or atoned for'. In the end the quarrel petered out at a dinner arranged by Samuel

[1] Moore, *Memoirs*, VII, 344.

Rogers, at which Campbell was also present.[1] It began awk-
wardly as Byron declared that he could dine only on biscuits
and soda-water, which had not been provided. He agreed,
however, to be content with cold potatoes and vinegar. The
insult was withdrawn and forgiven. What is more, the lasting
result was a friendship between the two protagonists, momen-
tous in literary history.

> My boat is on the shore,
>   And my bark is on the sea;
> But, before I go, Tom Moore,
>   Here's a double health to thee![2]

A realisation that it was impossible to fight a duel with Moore
without becoming his friend is not a bad preparation for
reading *Lalla Rookh*.

Lalla Rookh was a pot-boiler. Moore wrote it to make money,
and some very fortunate circumstances made the pot one that
he particularly wanted to bring to the boil. He entered into
negotiations with Longmans, being represented himself by a
friend, James Perry. Perry took a very strong line with them.[3]
'He was of the opinion', he said, 'that Mr Moore ought to
receive for his Poem the largest price that has been given, in
our day, for such a work. "That was", answered the Messrs
Longman, "three thousand guineas." "Exactly so," replied
Mr Perry, "and no less a sum ought he to receive." ' The

---

[1] Moore, *Memoirs*, II, 229. *The Works of Lord Byron with his Letters
and Journals, and his Life* by Thomas Moore (1832), II, 79–92. The
sting was really in Byron's note to these lines, 'The duel was prevented by the interference of the Magistracy; and on examination,
the balls of the pistols, like the courage of the combatants, were
found to have evaporated.' Byron omitted the reference to the
'courage of the combatants' and added a note on Moore's disavowal
of the story in the Fifth Edition of 1816. (*The Poetical Works of Lord
Byron*, ed. E. H. Coleridge (1898), I, 333–4.)

[2] Lord Byron, *Letters and Journals*, ed. R. E. Prothero (1898–
1904), IV, 148.

[3] Moore: *Memoirs*, II, 58, 119–20, 338, 355; IV, 23. *The Poetical
Works of Thomas Moore* (1840–1), VI, vi–viii.

publishers suggested that they might at least be allowed to see something of the work before agreeing to so generous an arrangement. Perry would have none of this.

> Of his judgment in the way of anticipating the popularity of a poem I can form no estimate [he wrote to Moore]. There may be a bookseller's knack; but I foresee an obvious inconvenience in this mode of treating. If after seeing the copy he should hesitate in giving the sum, or attempt to chaffer, he might wound your delicacy, and even injure the character of the work, by saying that he had refused it. I am not sure, therefore, my dear Sir, whether I ought not to tell you my own sentiment on the matter, which is frankly to decline the previous communication.[1]

'To the honour and glory of Romance,' as Moore put it,[2] Longmans agreed to pay a record price for a poem they were not to see. Three years later Moore wrote suggesting that they might like to see how he was getting on. 'We are certainly impatient for the perusal of the Poem,' came the reply, 'but solely for our gratification. Your sentiments are always honourable.'[3] Moore waited another year before sending them the manuscript. 'There has seldom, I think,' he was to write years later, 'occurred any transaction in which Trade and Poesy have shone out so advantageously in each other's eyes.'[4]

He found the writing of *Lalla Rookh* an uncommonly laborious task.

> It was [he said afterwards] far more through the encouraging suggestions of friends than from any confident promptings of my own ambition, I conceived the design of writing a Poem upon some Oriental subject, and of those quarto dimensions which Scott's successful publications in that form had then rendered the regular poetical standard.[5]

Inspiration was slow in coming. He tried several stories, some 'to the length of three or four hundred lines', and then aban-

---

[1] Moore, *Memoirs*, VIII, 178.   [2] Moore, *Poetical Works*, VI, vii.
[3] *Ibid.*, VI, viii.   [4] Moore, *Poetical Works*, VI, vi.
[5] *Ibid.*, VI, v–vi.

doned them in turn. Besides he was writing not only an oriental
tale, but something of a work of scholarship. The poem was,
he said, 'to form a store-house, as it were, of illustration purely
Oriental.'[1] And, 'I took the whole range of Oriental reading as
was accessible to me.[2] He aimed at attaining, and he claimed
to have achieved, 'the truth of the historian.'

But another difficulty intervened which he felt at first would
force him to abandon the poem. Byron trespassed on his field,
and in 1813 published *The Giaour*.

> I confess I feel rather downhearted about it [wrote Moore to
> a friend]. Never was anything more unlucky for me than
> Byron's invasion of this region, which when I entered it, was
> as yet untrodden, and whose chief charm consisted in the
> gloss and novelty of its features; but it will now be over-run
> with clumsy adventurers, and when I make my appearance
> instead of being a leader as I looked to be, I must dwindle
> into a humble follower — a Byronian. This is disheartening,
> and I sometimes doubt whether I shall publish it at all.[3]

Byron, however, brushed all this aside. 'Stick to the East,' he
wrote; 'the oracle, Staël, told me that it was the only poetical
policy.' But he went on to inform the luckless Moore that he
was intending to write a poem on the love of a Peri for a mortal.
Moore wrote miserably that he was well advanced on a story
with an exactly similar situation. Byron generously withdrew.[4]
Moore's poem, *The Peri's Daughter*, was actually one of those
that died in the making. The distressing and unintentional
competition continued. Byron published *The Bride of Abydos*
and Moore found to his dismay that 'not only in locality and
costume, but in plot and characters' it was uncomfortably like
a story he had finished and now had to abandon.[5]

---

[1] Moore, *Poetical Works*, VI, xvii.   [2] *Ibid.*, VI, xviii.
[3] Moore, *Memoirs*, VIII, 134.
[4] Byron: *Letters and Journals*, II, 255–6. 'Your Peri, my dear M., is
sacred and inviolable; I have no idea of touching the hem of her
petticoat.'
[5] 'Lord Byron's last poem *did give* me (I am sorry to tell you) a
deep wound in a very vital part — my story.' (*Memoirs*, VIII, 152.)

However, at last, in 1817, *Lalla Rookh* was published and received a rapturous reception. The oracle, Staël, who usually had her ear close to the ground, had been proved right. The East was indeed 'the only poetical policy'. What is remarkable is that Byron should have added, 'North, South and West have all been exhausted, but from the East, we have nothing but Southey's unsaleables.' One might well have imagined that the East was as exhausted as any other quarter of the globe. For centuries writers had been holding the gorgeous East in fee; Chaucer had written the *Tale of Cambuscan*, 'half-untold'; Marlowe the *History of Tamerlane*; Dryden the *Tragedy of Aureng-Zebe*; and Racine his *Bajazet*. But it was the publication of Galland's translation of the *Arabian Nights*, which appeared in an English version at the very beginning of the eighteenth century, followed in this country by the *Turkish Tales* in 1708, and the *Persian Tales* in 1714, which really began a new and most popular tradition in English literature.[1] What the East did for English writers at this time was to give them an excuse for kicking over the traces. Even Pope saw the possibilities. 'After reading the *Persian Tales* I had some thoughts of writing a Persian fable; in which I should have given full loose to description and imagination. It would have been a very wild thing if I had executed it, but might not have been unentertaining.'[2] It was, in fact, only too easy to bring the East to one's aid in romanticising a description. 'But instead of the rolling tide, the arched bridge, and the happy islands,' wrote Addison in the *Vision of Mirza*, 'I saw nothing but the long hollow valley of Bagdat, with oxen, sheep and camels grazing on the sides of it.' One suspects that he was actually standing on the North Downs, but Bagdat and the camels were enough to transform the scene. Not only was the East romantic; it was also wise. Essays in *The Spectator*, *The Guardian* and *The Rambler* proved that it could add both

[1] M. P. Conant, *The Oriental Tale in England in the Eighteenth Century* (New York, 1908).

[2] *Spence's Anecdotes*, ed. J. Underhill, 169, quoted in Conant, *op. cit.*, 244.

K

weight and charm to moralising or satire. *Zadig* and *Rasselas*, the *Lettres Persanes*, *A Letter from Xo-Ho* and *The Citizen of the World*, all showed in various ways how the most eminent writers could exploit the vein. 'Everything is Gothick, now it is Chinese,' wrote an essayist in 1753. But the two might be combined. Chatterton's *African Eclogues* were not far removed from Ossian. One of the *Turkish Tales* inspired *The Monk*, and in Beckford's *Vathek* we have at the same time one of the greatest of the Oriental romances and certainly the greatest of the romantic tales of terror.

But, it might be argued, all this was drawing on an Orient of the imagination. Since the days of Voltaire and Johnson there had developed a more realistic interest in the East. The great *Bibliothèque Orientale* of d'Herbelot, published as long ago as 1697, was reissued in an enlarged edition. William Robertson's *Disquisition concerning Ancient India* was complimented for bringing that country into 'the great road of history';[1] Sir William Jones brought European techniques of scholarship to bear on Indian literature; and between 1797 and 1799 Sir William Ouseley published his *Oriental Collections*, 'consisting of original essays and dissertations, translations, and miscellaneous papers, illustrating the history and antiquities, the arts, sciences and literature of Asia.' The wars with France in India, the exploits of Clive, the troubles of the East India Company, the trial of Warren Hastings, all gave Englishmen a new kind of interest in the East. Travellers' accounts of Persia and India began to supplant the Oriental romances.

It was only a beginning. Most Englishmen were still profoundly ignorant of the East. In 1790 Edward Ephraim Pote, son of the famous Eton bookseller, then in service with the East India Company, had despatched to King's College and Eton eight packing-cases of Oriental manuscripts, lettered A to H. The Provosts of the two Colleges were completely nonplussed by this unusual gift and it was eventually decided that

[1] D. Stewart, *Life of William Robertson* in W. Robertson, *Works* (1840), I, cxiii.

King's should have the boxes A to D, and Eton E to H. But Pote had filled them according to the convenience of packing. As a result, not only was the distribution entirely haphazard, but volumes of the same works were divided. There was no one at either College to know this and the two collections slumbered on the shelves of their respective libraries, uninvestigated for over a century. Readers still found the East romantic and mysterious, but they were becoming a little suspicious. Moore's extensive reading in the accounts of European travellers to the East enabled him to provide hundreds of footnotes verifying his local colour.[1] As we shall see, his tongue was in his cheek at times as he wrote *Lalla Rookh*, but not when he compiled the notes. For the rest of his life he was constantly referring with pride in his diary to instances of people congratulating him on the accuracy of his descriptions. This example will suffice. On 15 April 1820 he was in Paris: 'A lady (Mrs Skinner) had called upon us this morning, who said she had translated, while in India, the prose story of *Lalla Rookh*, for the amusement of her moonshee, and he was astonished at the accuracy of its costume.'[2] He was delighted that his poem was translated into so many languages, but he was never so elated as when

> Mr Stretch, whom I walked with yesterday, said he had been told by the nephew of the Persian ambassador, that *Lalla Rookh* had been translated into their language, and that the songs, (particularly that about Bendameere's Stream) are sung about everywhere; nor can they believe but that the whole work has been taken originally from some Persian manuscript.[3]

As Henry Luttrell, the most famous punster of the day, put it,

> I'm told, dear Moore, your lays are sung,
> (Can it be true, you lucky man ?)
> By moonlight, in the Persian tongue,
> Along the streets of Ispahan.[4]

[1] W. C. Brown, 'Thomas Moore and English Interest in the East' (*Studies in Philology* (1937), xxxiv).
[2] Moore, *Memoirs*, III, 111.   [3] *Ibid.*, III, 167.
[4] Moore, *Poetical Works*, VI, xxi.

The notes may seem tedious to us and more than a little ridiculous. But that was not the reaction of his contemporaries. What Moore called his 'accuracy as an Orientalist', his 'long and laborious collection of facts', impressed them greatly. Fortunately there were only a few who realised that the picture of the East in the poem, for all his labour, was as unreal as that in the conventional Oriental tales of the previous century, though one very astringent notice of the book in the *British Review* did point out that 'these miserable Turks and Greeks and Persians and Albanians make a figure only in the sickly pages of our Epicurean poets; there is scarcely an individual among them whom an Englishman of cleanly habits could endure by his side'.[1]

Moore had told Samuel Rogers at the end of 1815 that the poem was to have five tales and that it would take 'at the least six thousand lines to complete the plan'.[2] In fact it is rather shorter, about 5500 lines, and is made up of four tales, not five, entitled, *The Veiled Prophet of Khorassan, Paradise and the Peri, The Fire-Worshippers,* and *The Light of the Haram.* They are bound together by a prose narrative. This has come in for severe criticism. Byron said, 'I don't like the *prose* at all — at all.'[3] Stephen Gwynn in his life of Moore in the English Men of Letters series speaks of it as 'deplorable — sprightly beyond endurance'.[4] But Moore knew what he was about. Not only did he need the narrative to give some unity to the poem, but he could use it to lower the tone after the more rhapsodical passages, and, above all, to show the reader, in a way which I find distinctly attractive, that he was aware that the whole enterprise had its ridiculous aspect.

The prose story begins by telling how Abdalla, King of Lesser Bucharia, having abdicated in favour of his son, set out on a pilgrimage to Mecca and on the way visited Aurungzebe at Delhi. There it was decided that the Emperor's youngest daughter, the beautiful Lalla Rookh (a note informs us that the name means 'Tulip Cheek'), should marry the Prince of

[1] *British Review,* X (1817), 32.   [2] Moore, *Memoirs,* VIII, 205.
[3] Byron, *Letters and Journals,* IV, 169.   [4] *Op. cit.,* 86.

Bucharia and that 'the nuptials should be celebrated in the
enchanting valley of Cashmere'. The description of the
Princess's departure, firmly bolstered with footnotes, shows us
what we are to expect.

Seldom had the Eastern world seen a cavalcade so superb.
From the gardens in the suburbs to the Imperial palace, it
was one unbroken line of splendour. The gallant appearance
of the Rajahs and Mogul lords, distinguished by those
insignia of the Emperor's favour, the feathers of the egret of
Cashmere in their turbans, and the small silver-rimm'd
kettle-drums at the bows of their saddles; — the costly
armour of their cavaliers, who vied, on this occasion, with
the guards of the great Kedar Khan, in the brightness of
their silver battle-axes and the massiness of their maces of
gold;[1]

— the description is a very full one and this should serve. It
includes a reference to Fadladeen, Great Nazir or Chamberlain
of the Haram, who 'was a judge of everything, — from the
pencilling of a Circassian's eyelids to the deepest questions of
science and literature; from the mixture of a conserve of rose-
leaves to the composition of an epic poem'. By the time that the
introduction in prose is finished, some twelve pages, one has
been referred to Fryer's *Travels*, Elphinston's *Account of
Caubul*, Richardson's *Dissertation prefixed to his Dictionary*,
Scott's *Notes on the Bahardanush*, the Poems of Zadir in the
Moallakat, Bernier, Dow's *History of Hindostan*, the *Oriental
Collections*, Tavernier, Lieut. W. Franklin's *Account of the
present State of Delhi*, Pennant's *Hindostan*, Wilks' *South of
India*, Ouseley's *Persian Miscellanies*, Maurice's *Indian
Antiquities*, Calmet's *Dictionary* — Article on Bells,
d'Herbelot, Sir W. Jones on the *Gods of Greece, Italy, and
India*, and Turner's *Embassy*.

Before long the Princess and her attendants become bored
with the journey, when someone remembers that among the
attendants, who had been sent by the Prince of Bucharia to

---

[1] Moore, *Poetical Works*, VI, 8–9.

accompany them, was 'a young poet of Cashmere, much celebrated throughout the Valley for his manner of reciting the
Stories of the East'. The poet is summoned and

> the Princess, who had once in her life seen a poet from behind
> the screens of gauze in her Father's hall, and had conceived
> from that specimen no very favourable ideas of the Caste,
> expected but little in his new exhibition to interest her; —
> she felt inclined, however, to alter her opinion on the very
> first appearance of Feramorz.

And so

> the young Cashmerian ... having premised, with much
> humility, that the story he was about to relate was founded
> on the adventures of that Veiled Prophet of Khorassan, who,
> in the year of the Hegira 163, created such alarm throughout
> the Eastern Empire, made an obeisance to the Princess, and
> thus began:—
>
>> In that delightful Province of the Sun,
>> The first of Persian lands he shines upon,
>> Where all the loveliest children of his beam,
>> Flow'rets and fruits, blush over every stream,
>> And, fairest of all streams, the Murga roves
>> Among Merou's bright palaces and groves; —
>> There on that throne, to which the blind belief
>> Of millions rais'd him, sat the Prophet-Chief,
>> The Great Mokanna. O'er his features hung
>> The Veil, the Silver Veil, which he had flung
>> In mercy there, to hide from mortal sight
>> His dazzling brow, till men could bear its light.[1]

It is clearly not going to be possible to give even the plots
of all four stories and of the prose narrative; nor would it be
profitable to do so. The only way to refer poetry to your
judgment is to quote it. I shall dwell most on one story, the
first, and quote principally from one part of it, as it seems to
me to show Moore at his best. I should add that I know of only
one other critic who has shared my preference for *The Veiled*

---

[1] Moore, *Poetical Works*, VI, 19–20.

Prophet; that was the Rev. George Crabbe. But my business is not merely to be Counsel for the Defence, and I shall, therefore, feel it my duty — my embarrassing duty — to show you also in due course Moore at his worst.

Briefly, the first story tells how Mokanna, the Veiled Prophet, greets a new recruit, Azim, a young warrior who had been captured when fighting for the Caliph against the Byzantine Empire and released at the conclusion of a peace. There he had learnt the lesson of political liberty and, when he hears that Mokanna's banner carries the words, 'Freedom to the World', he enlists in his army. Mokanna explains to him that the world cannot be freed without much bloodshed. Any reader in Moore's own day would have realised that the story had a contemporary implication; he was speaking of the French Revolution and Mokanna was Napoleon Bonaparte. The subsequent discovery that the Prophet was actually a hideous tyrant would have seemed only too natural.

Among the members of Mokanna's Haram was Zelica. She and Azim had been lovers, but she had believed him killed in battle against the Greeks. She had agreed to enter the Haram of the Prophet on his promising her that at her death she would be the 'predestined bride' in Paradise of 'some brave youth', whom she assumed would certainly be Azim. And, watching from 'the Haram's curtain'd galleries', she had recognised the new recruit.

If the poem had not risen above the level of this introduction, I do not think that the most charitable critic, whatever its contemporary reputation, could refer to it as a forgotten masterpiece. But at this point Moore — or so it seems to me — received the benefit of a new source of inspiration. We are told how Mokanna, when Zelica had entered his Haram, had taken her

> To the dim charnel-house; — through all its steams
> Of damp and death, led only by those gleams
> Which foul Corruption lights, as with design
> To show the gay and proud *she* too can shine —
> And, passing on through upright ranks of Dead,

Which to the maiden, doubly craz'd by dread,
Seem'd, through the bluish death-light round them cast,
To move their lips in mutterings as she pass'd —
There, in that awful place, when each had quaff'd
And pledg'd in silence such a fearful draught,
Such — oh! the look and taste of that red bowl
Will haunt her till she dies — he bound her soul
By a dark oath, in hell's own language fram'd,
Never, while earth his mystic presence claim'd,
While the blue arch of day hung o'er them both,
Never, by that all-imprecating oath,
In joy or sorrow from his side to sever. —
She swore, and the wide charnel echoed, 'Never, never!'[1]

Zelica is summoned to the Prophet's presence. We see him now, not as the sacred prophet, but as the voluptuary and the destructive force that he really is. Soon he shows himself in his true colours and curses the race of men.

At length, with fiendish laugh, like that which broke
From Eblis at the Fall of Man, he spoke:—
'Yes, ye vile race, for hell's amusement given,
Too mean for earth, yet claiming kin with heaven;
God's images forsooth! — such gods as he
Whom India serves, the monkey deity; —
Ye creatures of a breath, proud things of clay,
To whom, if Lucifer, as grandams say,
Refus'd, though at the forfeit of heaven's light,
To bend in worship Lucifer was right!
Soon shall I plant his foot upon the neck
Of your foul race, and without fear or check,
Luxuriating in hate, avenge my shame,
My deep-felt, long-nurst loathing of man's name!
Soon at the head of myriads, blind and fierce
As hooded falcons, through the universe
I'll sweep my darkening, desolating way,
Weak man my instrument, curst man my prey!'[2]

[1] Moore, *Poetical Works*, VI, 38.
[2] *Ibid.*, VI, 45–7.

Mokanna's long speech ends with a splendid curse, of which one might have thought Moore was hardly capable.

> 'A Heav'n too ye must have, ye lords of dust, —
> A splendid Paradise, — pure souls, ye must:
> That Prophet ill sustains his holy call,
> Who finds not heav'ns to suit the tastes of all;
> Houris for boys, omniscience for sages,
> And wings and glories for all ranks and ages.
> Vain things! — as lust or vanity inspires,
> The heav'n of each is but what each desires,
> And, soul or sense, whate'er the object be,
> Man would be man to all eternity!
> So let him — Eblis! grant this crowning curse,
> But keep him what he is, no Hell were worse!'[1]

Zelica is then told how the prophet intends to corrupt Azim.

> 'All that my Haram boasts of bloom and wit,
> Of skill and charms, most rare and exquisite,
> Shall tempt the boy; — young Mirzala's blue eyes,
> Whose sleepy lid like snow on violets lies;
> Arouya's cheeks, warm as a spring-day sun,'

— we need not complete the list. One more is wanted,

> 'One who in every look joins every lure; . . .
> To crown the rich temptations of to-night;
> Such the refin'd enchantress that must be
> This hero's vanquisher, — and thou art she!'[2]

Zelica implores him to release her from the part, but she cannot escape.

> 'Hast thou forgot thy oath?' — . . . .
> 'Yes, my sworn bride, let others seek in bowers
> Their bridal place — the charnel vault was ours!
> Instead of scents and balms, for thee and me
> Rose the rich steams of sweet mortality;
> Gay, flickering death-lights shone while we were wed,
> And, for our guests, a row of goodly Dead,

[1] Moore, *Poetical Works*, VI, 48–9.   [2] *Ibid.*, VI, 51–3.

(Immortal spirits in their time, no doubt,)
From reeking shrouds upon the rite look'd out!'[1]

Finally Mokanna exclaims,

'And now thou seest my *soul's* angelic hue,
'Tis time these *features* were uncurtain'd too; —
This brow, whose light — oh rare celestial light!
Hath been reserv'd to bless thy favour'd sight;
These dazzling eyes, before whose shrouded might
Thou'st seen immortal Man kneel down and quake —
Would that they *were* heaven's lightnings for his sake!
But turn and look — then wonder, if thou wilt,
That I should hate, should take revenge, by guilt,
Upon the hand, whose mischief or whose mirth
Sent me thus maim'd and monstrous upon earth;
And on that race who, though more vile they be
Than mowing apes, are demi-gods to me!
Here — judge if hell, with all its powers to damn,
Can add one curse to the foul thing I am!' —
He rais'd the veil — the Maid turn'd slowly round,
Look'd at him — shriek'd — and sunk upon the ground![2]

And with that Feramorz's recital for the night ended.

I think there can be little doubt what was Moore's inspiration in writing this part of the story. I do not suppose that it
can be proved that he had read Beckford's *Vathek* before he
wrote *Lalla Rookh*. He had certainly read it later in his life and
it must be probable that he had done so as a young man.
Perhaps the references in this section of the poem to Eblis
are significant. Certainly Moore could not achieve the horrors
of the hall of Eblis and his characterisation is far weaker than
Beckford's. But he showed himself able to do what Beckford
had done and combine the two romantic traditions of the
eighteenth century. And there are other echoes too. For the
mocking tone, which one hears at times, mocking himself and
his readers, recalls the poems of a greater writer than Beckford.

1 Moore, *Poetical Works*, VI, 58.
2 *Ibid.*, VI, 59–60.

> So let him — Eblis! grant this crowning curse,
> But keep him what he is, no Hell were worse!

Byron might have written those lines.

The prose narrative, which at this point breaks into the poem, does all that is required of it. Moore needed to slacken the tension, for the next night's recital starts in an altogether different tone. Moore here does something Beckford had not attempted and succeeds brilliantly in producing the impression of the silences and the sounds of Azim's strange, dreamlike encounter with the ladies of Mokanna's Haram.

> Meanwhile, through vast illuminated halls,
> Silent and bright, where nothing but the falls
> Of fragrant waters, gushing with cool sound
> From many a jasper fount, is heard around,
> Young Azim roams bewilder'd, — nor can guess
> What means this maze of light and loneliness.
> Here, the way leads, o'er tesselated floors
> Or mats of Cairo, through long corridors,
> Where, rang'd in cassolets and silver urns,
> Sweet wood of aloe or of sandal burns.[1]

He watches in silence the goldfish in the fountains and the birds in their cages; then he recalls his purpose and decides,

> 'this glare of luxury
> Is but to tempt, to try the eaglet gaze
> Of my young soul — shine on, 'twill stand the blaze!'
> So thought the youth; — but, ev'n while he defied
> The witching scene, he felt its witchery glide
> Through ev'ry sense. The perfume breathing round,
> Like a pervading spirit; — the still sound
> Of falling waters, lulling as the song
> Of Indian bees at sunset, when they throng
> Around the fragrant Nilica, and deep
> In its blue blossoms hum themselves to sleep;
> And music, too — dear music! that can touch
> Beyond all else the soul that loves it much —

[1] Moore, *Poetical Works*, VI, 67–8.

> Now heard far off, so far as but to seem
> Like the faint, exquisite music of a dream.[1]

He sinks down on a couch and — inevitably — thinks of Zelica.
But his musings are interrupted.

> While thus he thinks, still nearer on the breeze
> Come those delicious, dream-like harmonies,
> Each note of which but adds new, downy links
> To the soft chain in which his spirit sinks.
> He turns him tow'rd the sound, and far away
> Through a long vista, sparkling with the play
> Of countless lamps, — like the rich track which Day
> Leaves on the waters, when he sinks from us,
> So long the path, its light so tremulous; —
> He sees a group of female forms advance,
> Some chain'd together in the mazy dance
> By fetters, forg'd in the green sunny bowers,
> As they were captives to the King of Flowers;
> And some disporting round, unlink'd and free,
> Who seem'd to mock their sisters' slavery;
> And round and round them still, in wheeling flight
> Went, like gay moths about a lamp at night.[2]

The dance breaks up,

> Till silently dispersing, one by one,
> Through many a path, that from the chamber leads
> To gardens, terraces, and moonlight meads,
> Their distant laughter comes upon the wind,
> And but one trembling nymph remains behind.[3]

The girl sings a song which was as much applauded as anything
else in the poem; it was the song which the nephew of the
Persian ambassador said was sung in Persia. I am afraid that
we shall probably feel differently. We have heard these
anapaests too often; the magic is broken and we are back once
more in the Regency drawing-room with Moore at the piano
and not a dry eye in the company.

[1] Moore, *Poetical Works*, VI, 72-3.
[2] *Ibid.*, VI, 74-5.
[3] *Ibid.*, VI, 76.

There's a bower of roses by Bendemeer's stream,
   And the nightingale sings round it all the day long;
In the time of my childhood 'twas like a sweet dream,
   To sit in the roses and hear the birds' song.

That bower and its music I never forget,
   But oft when alone, in the bloom of the year,
I think — is the nightingale singing there yet?
   Are the roses still bright by the calm Bendemeer?[1]

It is hardly necessary to quote any more.

Other girls come in and dance more gaily; more songs are sung. Azim leaps from his couch and moves through walls covered with pictures of the famous beauties of Moslem story, the Queen of Saba, Zuleika, and Mary, the beloved of Mohammed. I cannot forbear adding one of Moore's footnotes — we should not forget that these notes have been with us all the time — 'The particulars of Mahomet's amour with Mary, the Coptic girl, in justification of which he added a new chapter to the Koran, may be found in *Gagnier's Notes on Abulfeda*, p. 151.'[2] I must admit to finding a wholly irreverent delight in these notes, but that is not what Moore meant one to find. They give the poem for me an unfair advantage.

Azim passes

               these pictur'd stories by,
And hasten'd to a casement, where the light
Of the calm moon came in, and freshly bright
The fields without were seen, sleeping as still
As if no life remain'd in breeze or rill.
Here paus'd he, while the music, now less near,
Breath'd with a holier language on his ear,
As though the distance, and that heavenly ray
Through which the sounds came floating, took away
All that had been too earthly in the lay.[3]

And then,

[1] Moore, *Poetical Works*, VI, 77–8.   [2] *Ibid.*, VI, 85.
[3] *Ibid.*, VI, 85–6.

The song is hush'd, the laughing nymphs are flown,
And he is left, musing of bliss, alone; —
Alone? — no not alone — that heavy sigh,
That sob of grief, which broke from some one nigh —
Whose could it be? — alas! is misery found
Here, even here, on this enchanted ground?[1]

It is, of course, Zelica. The meeting between the lovers was
more than Moore could manage. Their speeches are much too
long. Zelica tells of her appalling guilt,

Enough, that we are parted — that there rolls
A flood of headlong fate between our souls,
Whose darkness severs me as wide from thee
As hell from heav'n, to all eternity![2]

But Azim declares that he forgives her and implores her to
escape with him. Zelica gives in,

'Oh yes, I'll fly with thee — '
                       Scarce had she said
These breathless words, when a voice deep and dread
As that of Monker, waking up the dead
From their first sleep — so startling 'twas to both —
Rang through the casement near, 'Thy oath! Thy oath!'

She is powerless.

'Tis he, and I am his — all, all is o'er —
Go — fly this instant, or thou'rt ruin'd too —
My oath, my oath, oh God! 'tis all too true,
True as the worm in this cold heart it is —
I am Mokanna's bride — his, Azim, his —
The Dead stood round us, while I spoke that vow,
Their blue lips echo'd it — I hear them now!
Their eyes glar'd on me.

She tears herself from Azim and

Flew up through that long avenue of light,
Fleetly as some dark, ominous bird of night,
Across the sun, and soon was out of sight![3]

[1] Moore, *Poetical Works*, VI, 87.   [2] *Ibid.*, VI, 94.
[3] *Ibid.*, VI, 95–7.

Lalla Rookh [the Prose narrative continues immediately] could think of nothing all day but the misery of these two lovers. Her gaiety was gone, and she looked pensively even upon Fadladeen. She felt too, without knowing why, a sort of uneasy pleasure in imagining that Azim must have been just such a youth as Feramorz.

The story was finished the next night and I do not think that I need give much more than the barest narrative. It opens with a description of a tremendous battle in which Mokanna all but defeats the Caliph, but the tide is turned by the incredible bravery of one warrior, who is Azim. Mokanna flees to his last stronghold of Neksheb, taking only Zelica with him of all his Haram, and is closely besieged. A last, desperate sortie fails and, while Greek fire,

> red-hot globes, that opening as they mount,
> Discharge, as from a kindled Naphtha fount,
> Showers of consuming fire o'er all below,[1]

which gave Moore an opportunity for the longest of all his notes, the Veiled Prophet holds his last banquet. There he unveils and shows his faithful companions his face,

> Not the long promis'd light, the brow, whose beaming
> Was to come forth, all conquering, all redeeming,
> But features horribler than Hell e'er trac'd
> On its own brood.[2]

At the banquet all his companions are poisoned and the prophet leaps into a bath of liquid fire. (In fairness to Moore, I ought to say that all this comes faithfully from d'Herbelot.) Zelica is left alone. She puts on the Silver Veil as the Caliph's army bursts in, and then throws herself on Azim's spear. She dies in his arms. Azim lives on for many years, praying by her grave, until

> His soul had seen a Vision, while he slept;
> She, for whose spirit he had pray'd and wept
> So many years, had come to him, all drest

---

[1] Moore, *Poetical Works*, VI, 127.   [2] *Ibid.*, VI, 133.

In angel smiles, and told him she was blest!
For this the old man breath'd his thanks, and died. —
And there, upon the banks of that lov'd tide,
He and his Zelica sleep side by side.[1]

The story of the Veiled Prophet of Khorassan being ended,
they were now doomed to hear Fadladeen's criticisms upon it.
[The prose narrative begins at once with these words] 'In
order', said he, importantly swinging about his chaplet of
pearls, 'to convey with clearness my opinion of the story this
young man has related, it is necessary to take a review of all
the stories that have ever — ' — 'My good Fadladeen!'
exclaimed the Princess, interrupting him, 'we really do not
deserve that you give yourself so much trouble.'

Fadladeen is thus constrained to give a briefer criticism
than he had intended, although, as Moore is enjoying himself,
it is fairly thorough. A few extracts will suffice us.

The chief personages in the story were, if he rightly understood them, an ill-favoured gentleman, with a veil over his face;
— a young lady, whose reason went and came, according as it
suited the poet's convenience to be sensible or otherwise; —
and a youth in one of those hideous Bucharian bonnets, who
took the aforesaid gentleman in a veil for a Divinity.

'From such materials', said he 'what can be expected? —
after rivalling each other in long speeches and absurdities . . .
our friend in a veil jumps into a tub of aquafortis; the young
lady dies in a set speech, whose only recommendation is that
it is her last; and the lover lives on to a good old age, for the
laudable purpose of seeing her ghost, which he at length
happily accomplishes, and expires. . . .'

Then, as to the versification, it was, to say no worse of it,
execrable: it had neither the copious flow of Ferdosi, the
sweetness of Hafez, nor the sententious march of Sadi; but
appeared to him, in the uneasy heaviness of its movements, to
have been modelled upon the gait of a very tired dromedary. . . .

[1] Moore, *Poetical Works*, VI, 142.

'Notwithstanding the observations which I have thought it my duty to make, [he concludes] it is by no means my wish to discourage the young man: — so far from it, indeed, that if he will but totally alter his style of writing and thinking, I have very little doubt that I shall be vastly pleased with him.'[1]

We must allow that the humour is ponderous; we have suffered much from this kind of burlesque since Moore's day. But at least it takes a good deal of the wind out of our sails. The point of the criticism is surely, however, that Fadladeen is Jeffrey. Moore is laughing at his friend and also, in the most disarming way, having his revenge for the review which had first brought them together.

The next story is entitled *Paradise and the Peri*. It is, I suppose, the best known of the four and it was greatly admired. I admit that I find both narrative and language very embarrassing. The story is a very simple one. A Peri, barred from Paradise like all her race, is told by the Guardian Angel at the gate,

> One hope is thine.
> 'Tis written in the Book of Fate,
> '*The Peri yet may be forgiven*
> *Who brings to this Eternal Gate*
> *The Gift that is most dear to Heaven!*'[2]

The Peri brings first the last drop of blood shed by a hero, who dies in battle, defending his country, but is told

> 'holier far
> Than ev'n this drop the boon must be,
> That opes the Gates of Heav'n for thee!'[3]

She then visits a plague-stricken city and finds a young man dying and alone, but comforted by the thought that his mistress is away and safe. She comes to him, however, and he dies in her arms. The Peri

> stole
> The farewell sigh of that vanishing soul,

---

[1] Moore, *Poetical Works*, VI, 143–9.
[2] *Ibid.*, VI, 158.   [3] *Ibid.*, VI, 164.

and bears it to Paradise, only to be told that

> 'holier far
> Than ev'n this sigh the boon must be
> That opes the Gates of Heav'n for thee.'[1]

And now in Syria, in the vale of Balbec, she finds a child, lying at rest among roses. A warrior, an utterly evil man, comes up. What happens will have to be told in Moore's own words.

> But hark! the vesper call to prayer,
>   As slow the orb of daylight sets,
> Is rising sweetly on the air,
>   From Syria's thousand minarets!
> The boy has started from the bed
> Of flowers, where he had laid his head,
> And down upon the fragrant sod
>   Kneels, with his forehead to the south,
> Lisping th' eternal name of God
>   From Purity's own cherub mouth,
> And looking, while his hands and eyes
> Are lifted to the glowing skies,
> Like a stray babe of Paradise,
> Just lighted on the flowery plain,
> And seeking for its home again.[2]

We are spared nothing. The 'wretched man' now prays too; he weeps 'blest tears of soul-felt penitence'; the Peri takes

> the tear that, warm and meek,
> Dew'd that repentant sinner's cheek,

aloft to Paradise and is admitted. As if that were not enough, Moore then allowed himself some lines, in the Peri's song in Paradise, which make any parodies of his poetic style completely unnecessary.

> Joy, joy, for ever! my task is done —
> The Gates are pass'd, and Heaven is won!
> Oh, am I not happy? I am, I am —
>   To thee, sweet Eden! how dark and sad

---

[1] Moore, *Poetical Works*, VI, 175.
[2] *Ibid.*, VI, 180–1.

Are the diamond turrets of Shadukiam,
  And the fragrant bowers of Amberabad!

Farewell, ye odours of Earth, that die
Passing away like a lover's sigh; —
My feast is now of the Tooba Tree,
Whose scent is the breath of Eternity![1]

Fadladeen does his best for us. ' "And this", said the Great
Chamberlain, "is poetry! this flimsy manufacture of the brain,
which in comparison with the lofty and durable monuments of
genius, is as the gold filigree-work of Zamara beside the eternal
architecture of Egypt!" ' But Jeffrey in the *Edinburgh Review*
thought otherwise. *Paradise and the Peri*, he said, 'is full of
spirit, elegance and beauty; and though slight enough in its
structure, breathes throughout a most pure and engaging
morality.'[2]

The cavalcade now reaches Lahore and it is learnt that the
young king is coming to meet them in the Vale of Cashmere.
Lalla Rookh then realises that 'she was in love, irretrievably
in love, with young Feramorz' and she resolves to see him no
more. However, one night they sit down under the ruins of an
ancient Fire-Temple. No one, not even Fadladeen, can say
what it was; one of the ladies suggests that Feramorz might
satisfy their curiosity; and before Lalla Rookh can intervene
he is summoned. He tells them the Story of the Fire-
Worshippers.

It appears to have been at this point that Moore began to
realise that he was not going to be able to finish the poem, in
spite of the very favourable arrangements agreed on between
Trade and Poesy. But, if he had been unlucky before, he now
benefited from a fortunate breeze.

At last the thought occurred to me of founding a story on
the fierce struggle so long maintained between the Ghebers,
or ancient Fire-worshippers of Persia, and their haughty

[1] Moore, *Poetical Works*, VI, 184–5.
[2] Francis Jeffrey, *Contributions to the Edinburgh Review* (1844), III,
216.

Moslem masters. From that moment, a new and deep interest in my whole task took possession of me. The cause of tolerance was again my inspiring theme; and the spirit that had spoken in the melodies of Ireland soon found itself at home in the East.[1]

I suppose we must take Moore's word for it. The story is a simple one. A warrior, Hafed, visits by night a maiden, Hinda, the daughter of a Moslem general fighting against the Fire worshippers of Persia, who are making a last desperate defence of their religion and their native land. He tells her that he must leave her and she discovers that he is one of the rebels. Before the attack on the rebel's last stronghold, her father sends her away on a ship and she is captured by them. She recognises her lover as their dreaded leader. In spite of her warnings (for her father had told her that he had the help of a traitor) the castle is taken; Hafed immolates himself on a funeral pyre and Hinda throws herself into the sea. No one reading the poem now, without the clue provided by Moore himself, would be likely to be reminded of the United Irishmen or the struggle for Catholic Emancipation. Moore, it is true, was always loyal to the cause of the Catholics in Ireland and later in life he was to support O'Connell and the Repealers, though with a good many reservations, but he never ventured into dangerous political waters. There were lines in the poem, however, which, in the days after the Congress of Vienna, might have seemed to show that Moore was on the side of Revolution.

> Rebellion! foul, dishonouring word,
> 　Whose wrongful blight so oft has stain'd
> The holiest cause that tongue or sword
> 　Of mortal ever lost or gain'd.
> How many a spirit, born to bless,
> 　Hath sunk beneath that withering name,
> Whom but a day's, an hour's success,
> 　Had wafted to eternal fame![2]

[1] Moore, *Poetical Works*, VI, xvi.
[2] *Ibid.*, VI, 235.

and,

>   Such were tales, that won belief,
>   And such the colouring Fancy gave
>   To a young, warm, and dauntless Chief, —
>   One who, no more than mortal brave,
>   Fought for the land his soul ador'd,
>   For happy homes and altars free, —
>   His only talisman, the sword,
>   His only spell-word, Liberty![1]

At any rate Byron ranked it first of the four poems.[2]

It was not the lines inspired by Catholic Emancipation, however, that had most to do with the success of *The Fire-Worshippers*. If only we could surrender ourselves to the romance of Moore's Oriental background and to the skill of his rhythms, we might be able to recapture some of the enthusiasm with which this poem was first read.

>   The nightingale now bends her flight
>   From the high trees, where all the night
>   She sung so sweet, with none to listen;
>   And hides her from the morning star
>   Where thickets of pomegranate glisten
>   In the clear dawn, — bespangled o'er
>   With dew, whose night-drops would not stain
>   The best and brightest scimitar
>   That ever youthful Sultan wore
>   On the first morning of his reign.[3]
>
>   How calm, how beautiful comes on
>   The stilly hour, when storms are gone;
>   When warring winds have died away,
>   And clouds, beneath the glancing ray,
>   Melt off, and leave the land and sea
>   Sleeping in bright tranquillity, —

[1] Moore, *Poetical Works*, VI, 237.

[2] One cannot be quite sure of Byron's real opinion of *Lalla Rookh*. Hobhouse wrote, 'Nevertheless I have heard him express a very different opinion of Tommy's tale.'

[3] Moore, *Poetical Works*, VI, 231.

Fresh as if Day again were born,
Again upon the lap of Morn![1]

The poem ends with what Jeffrey called 'a sort of choral dirge, of great elegance and beauty'.

Farewell — farewell to thee, Araby's daughter!
(Thus warbled a Peri beneath the dark sea,)
No pearl ever lay, under Oman's green water,
More pure in its shell than thy Spirit in thee.

Oh! fair as the sea-flower close to thee growing,
How light was thy heart till Love's witchery came,
Like the wind of the south o'er a summer lute blowing,
And hush'd all its music, and wither'd its frame!

But long, upon Araby's green sunny highlands,
Shall maids and their lovers remember the doom
Of her, who lies sleeping among the Pearl Islands,
With nought but the sea-star to light up her tomb.[2]

I feel that I must allow myself two more of the notes. Moore, himself, would not have wanted them to be forgotten.

'This wind (the Samoor) so softens the strings of lutes, that they can never be tuned while it lasts.' — *Stephen's Persia*.

'One of the greatest curiosities found in the Persian Gulf is a fish which the English call Star-fish. It is circular, and at night very luminous, resembling the full moon surrounded by rays.' — *Mirza Abu Taleb*.

The best-known lines — and they can hardly be omitted — come early in the poem, when Hinda realises that she will never see Hafed again.

We part — for ever part — to-night!
I knew, I knew, it *could* not last —
'Twas bright, 'twas heavenly, but 'tis past!

---

[1] Moore, *Poetical Works*, VI, 268–9.

[2] Moore, *Poetical Works*, VI, 319–20. 'Araby's green sunny highlands' is rather surprising. Perhaps Moore was then thinking of Ireland.

Oh! ever thus, from childhood's hour,
I've seen my fondest hopes decay;
I never loved a tree or flower,
    But 'twas the first to fade away.

I never nurs'd a dear gazelle,
    To glad me with its soft black eye,
But when it came to know me well,
    And love me, it was sure to die![1]

The sentimentality lies even more in the rhythm than in the words. But what shocks us most in these lines is that they come at a moment of passion, when a girl is saying farewell for ever to her lover. Moore's lapses of taste are astonishing. By now, however, we should be ready for any verdict pronounced by contemporaries on any poem. Sir Walter Scott held that *The Fire-Worshippers* was 'the best poem written by any of the living poets'.[2]

Of the last of the stories, *The Light of the Haram*, which is the shortest and least serious, I shall quote only its opening lines. As one reads them, one must at least admire Moore's extraordinary facility.

Who has not heard of the Vale of Cashmere,
    With its roses the brightest that earth ever gave,
Its temples, and grottos, and fountains as clear
    As the love-lighted eyes that hang over their wave?

Oh! to see it at sunset, — when warm o'er the Lake
    Its splendour at parting a summer eve throws,
Like a bride, full of blushes, when ling'ring to take
    A last look at her mirror at night ere she goes! —
When the shrines through the foliage are gleaming half shown,
And each hallows the hour by some rites of its own.
Here the music of pray'r from a minaret swells,
    Here the Magian his urn, full of perfume, is swinging,
And here, at the altar, a zone of sweet bells
    Round the waist of some fair Indian dancer is ringing.

[1] Moore, *Poetical Works*, VI, 217–18.
[2] Moore, *Memoirs*, III, 263.

Or see it by moonlight, — when mellowly shines
The light o'er its palaces, gardens, and shrines;
When the water-falls gleam, like a quick fall of stars,
And the nightingale's hymn from the Isle of Chenars
Is broken by laughs and light echoes of feet
From the cool, shining walks where the young people meet.[1]

The prose narrative had yet to be completed. We are not likely to find the dénouement unexpected. The cavalcade reaches the Valley and the bride meets her husband.

> Immediately upon the entrance of Lalla Rookh in the saloon, the monarch descended from his throne to meet her; but scarcely had he time to take her hand in his, when she screamed with surprise, and fainted at his feet. It was Feramorz himself that stood before her! . . . Of the happiness of the King and Queen of Bucharia, after such a beginning, there can be but little doubt; and among the lesser symptoms, it is recorded of Lalla Rookh, that, to the day of her death, in memory of their delightful journey, she never called the King by any other name than Feramorz.[2]

These are the concluding words, and with them Moore holds out his hand to countless Victorian novelists to come.

This may help us to understand why *Lalla Rookh* was so popular. Only about twenty years before it was published, English literature had suddenly produced a new genre, the verse story. When one remembers Chaucer, Gower and Lydgate, and *The Mirror for Magistrates*, it may seem strange that for two centuries it had been so neglected. No doubt the rise of the novel helped to revive it.[3] This new mould for poetry was used by all the leading poets of the early nineteenth century. Moore, then, wrote in a poetic form which was still quite new, but had already proved its popularity. At the same time readers found its setting and the oriental allusions exciting. He had one obvious precursor. Even Byron had to admit that

[1] Moore, *Poetical Works*, VII, 12.
[2] *Ibid.*, VII, 68–9.
[3] More important, probably, were Percy's *Reliques* and the interest they created in the Ballad.

'Southey's unsaleables' came from the East. One might imagine that his *Thalaba* and *The Curse of Kehama* were one of Moore's sources of inspiration, but he does not seem to have been in the least interested in them. And there is a world of difference between Southey's portentously solemn poems and the lines that floated out of Moore's 'sparkling, anacreontic mouth'.

There was life in the Orient yet; it was to inspire Matthew Arnold, FitzGerald and James Elroy Flecker. For us — or, at least, for most of us — its charm has faded, but it was not so very long ago that it did. Flecker's *Hassan* — it seems hardly credible now — was published in the same year as *The Waste Land*. At the time when *Lalla Rookh* was written, the only criticism was that Moore gave his readers rather too much of a good thing. Even Lord John Russell, who held that 'of English lyric poets, Moore is surely the greatest', had to admit that *Lalla Rookh* was 'too sumptous a feast'. It is significant that its critics constantly have recourse to similes from confectionery. Lamb spoke of it as 'very rich plum cake'; Hazlitt compared it to strawberry-ice; and George Saintsbury referred to its 'meringue-like quality'.

Nothing is more difficult than to recapture the excitement with which a poem, which has dated, was read or heard when it first appeared. 'Repeated my Neapolitan verses to Lady Fielding and Fielding,' wrote Moore in his diary in 1821; 'she said they were like sparks of fire running through her in all directions.'[1] At that time the Romantic Movement in England was young, Moore, with Sir Walter Scott, made it respectable. As Moore was leaving the theatre once in Paris with Madame de Flahault, the Duchesse de Raguse came over and whispered to ask her if it was M. Walter Scott on her arm. 'No, it was Mr Moore.' '*Ah! c'est la même chose, c'est* Lalla Rookh *que j'adore.*'[2] I find it an interesting exercise to take some of the fragments left by Shelley in his last years and to imagine that I had come across them in *Lalla Rookh*. Often I feel that they would pass unnoticed. And then one reads lines which Moore could never have written,

[1] Moore, *Memoirs*, III, 217.   [2] *Ibid.*, III, 111.

> One word is too often profaned
> For me to profane it.
>
> When the lamp is shattered,
> The light in the dust lies dead.

But Shelley was not read by the Fieldings.

The Fire-Worshippers may have impressed those who were on Shelley's side. Moore was proud to learn that this story had been translated, not merely into the Polish language, but 'in a Polish sense'.[1] But that was not how *Lalla Rookh* was generally received. Perhaps the most devastating criticism of Moore — all the more so for being quite unconscious — was made by Haydon, when he described the rival, who for a time stole the heart of his beloved Mary, as 'a fascinating young man, full of Moore and light reading'.[2] It is significant of the circles in which the poem was popular that at once race-horses began to be named after Lalla Rookh, Nourmahal, and other favourite characters in it. We can learn most of what it meant to its contemporaries from its extraordinary apotheosis.

In 1822 the Grand Duke Nicholas visited Berlin with his wife.[3] He was soon to be Czar, the Czar of the Decembrist Revolution, who, on hearing the news of the rising in Paris in 1848, was to storm into a ball-room, shouting, 'Gentlemen! saddle your horses; France is a republic again.' The visit marked the heyday of the Holy Alliance. The guests amused themselves by acting a Divertissement of *Lalla Rookh*, with Tableaux Vivants and songs. The Grand Duke himself took the part of the King of Bucharia — and, therefore, of Feramorz; the Grand Duchess that of Lalla Rookh; Aurung-zebe was played by the brother of the King of Prussia; Abdallah, the brother of the King of Bucharia, by Ernst August, Duke of Cumberland. Knights and Ladies of Bucharia, Ladies of Cashmere, Knights and Ladies dancing at the Feast of Roses

---

[1] Moore, *Memoirs*, VII, 196.

[2] *The Diary of Benjamin Robert Haydon*, ed. W. B. Pope (Cambridge, Mass., 1960), II, 284.

[3] Moore, *Memoirs*, III, 203–17. *Poetical Works*, VI, xxiii–xxvi.

gave parts to a hundred and fifty members of the Court. When
the performance was over, the Grand Duchess exclaimed with a
sigh, 'Is it, then, all over? are we now at the close of all that
has given us so much delight? and lives there no poet who will
impart to others, and to future times, some notion of the
happiness we have enjoyed this evening?' What could one of
the Knights of Cashmere do but to promise to translate 'the
Poem itself in the measure of the original'? He was Baron la
Motte Fouqué, the author of *Undine*. He was as good as his
word and Moore heard to his delight that the Grand Duchess
always carried about with her 'two copies of *Lalla Rookh*
most splendidly bound and studded with precious stones'.[1]
That, metaphorically speaking, is how we should read it. As a
period piece — and I do not think that our generation can
regard it as anything else — it is worth reading. Perhaps the
time will come when *Omar Khayyam* and *Hassan* have been
forgotten so long that they will no longer trouble us, and then,
provided that the demands we make of poetry are not too high,
Lalla Rookh may be found to have some rights of its own.

[1] Moore, *Memoirs*, III, 262.

VI

Philip James Bailey
Festus

In 1829 Francis Jeffrey in the *Edinburgh Review* contemplated with little confidence the probable future reputation of the poet who, in his opinion, was 'beyond all comparison the most touching and accomplished writer of occasional verses that our literature has yet to boast of' — Mrs Felicia Hemans, author of *Casabianca* ('The boy stood on the burning deck').

We have seen too much [he declared] of the perishable nature of modern literary fame, to venture to predict to Mrs Hemans that hers will be immortal, or even of very long duration. Since the beginning of our critical career we have seen a vast deal of beautiful poetry pass into oblivion, in spite of my feeble efforts to recall or retain it in remembrance. The tuneful quartos of Southey are already little better than lumber; and the rich melodies of Keats and Shelley, and the fantastical emphasis of Wordsworth, and the plebeian pathos of Crabbe, are melting fast from our field of vision. The novels of Scott have put out his poetry. Even the splendid strains of Moore are fading into distance and dimness, except when they have been married to immortal music; and the blazing star of Byron himself is receding from its place of pride. We need say nothing of Milman and Croly, and Atherstone, and Hood, and a legion of others, who, with no ordinary gifts of taste and fancy, have not so properly survived their fame, as been excluded by some hard fatality from what seemed their just inheritance. The two who have longest withstood this rapid withering of the laurel, and with the least mark of decay on their branches, are Rogers and

Campbell, neither of them, it may be remarked, voluminous writers, and both distinguished rather for the fine taste and consummate elegance of their writings, than for the fiery passion, and disdainful vehemence, which seemed for a time to be so much more in favour with the public.[1]

During the next ten years there was very little to encourage anyone anxious for the future of English poetry. Those in Jeffrey's roll of honour who survived produced little or nothing. Sir Henry Taylor's play, *Philip van Artevelde*, was the only poetic work of the period generally accepted as a masterpiece, a work which would never be forgotten. It was a decade of Juvenilia, when the first publications appeared of Tennyson, Browning and Miss Elizabeth Barrett. Among these was an anonymous poetic drama of a little over 8000 lines, entitled *Festus*, published in 1839. It received a mixed reception. The *Athenaeum* considered it 'a mere plagiarism from the *Faust* of Goethe, with all its impiety and scarcely any of its poetry'. But there were other more favourable judgments. Bulwer Lytton thought it 'a most remarkable and magnificent production'. James Montgomery (the well-known hymn-writer, often called 'Antediluvian' Montgomery from his epic, *The World before the Flood*, and to be distinguished from Robert Montgomery, so ruthlessly slaughtered by Macaulay in the *Edinburgh Review*) said that on reading it 'one feels as if one had "eaten of the insane root that takes the reason prisoner" in many passages; or rather "of the tree of knowledge of good and evil", with strange elevations of spirit, and stranger misgivings, alternately glowing and shivering through the bosom'. Ebenezer Elliott, the Corn-Law Rhymer, held that it had 'poetry enough for fifty poets'. Robert Hengist Horne (better known as 'Orion' Horne from his epic of that name) spoke of its 'unrepressed vigour of imagination, splendour of imagery and passion of poetry', in his book, *The Spirit of the Age*, which he wrote with the help of Miss Elizabeth Barrett, another admirer. As for Harrison Ainsworth, who brought out *The*

---

[1] Francis Jeffrey, *Contributions to the 'Edinburgh Review'*, III, 296–7.

Tower of London the next year, he concluded that the author's 'place will be among the first, if not the first, of our native poets'.[1] The poem was quickly noted on the other side of the Atlantic. Margaret Fuller, the lady who declared, 'I accept the Universe!' drawing Carlyle's comment, 'Gad, you'd better,' reviewed it favourably and at length in the *Dial*, the transcendentalist review she had just founded in Boston. 'It speaks', she said, 'from soul to soul.' Her friend Emerson, however, was more cautious.[2]

In spite of this encouraging reception by some not inconsiderable writers, the poem remained for a few years comparatively unknown. Then, in 1845, there appeared a second edition, revised and lengthened — it was now nearly 13,000 lines. The authorship was now acknowledged. It was by Philip James Bailey, Barrister at Law. This time it attracted a great deal of attention. Tennyson wrote to FitzGerald, 'I have just got *Festus*; order it and read. You will most likely find it a great bore, but there really are *very grand* things in *Festus*.'[3] 'The magnanimous old dog', FitzGerald was to write thirty years later, 'tried to force Bailey's *Festus* down my throat.'[4] He was not the only sufferer.

He spent a good part of the last months of the year [1846] in London, being much fêted and dined, [Charles Tennyson, the poet's grandson, tells us] and expressing great admiration for that now forgotten poem, Bailey's *Festus*, which he declared contained many grand things — grander than anything he himself had written. At one dinner-party the company, who doubted his sincerity, not knowing his singular magnanimity about the works of his contemporaries, challenged him to repeat a line of Bailey's poem, whereupon he silenced criticism by quoting:

[1] Notices of the first edition of *Festus*, printed at the end of the Second Edition of 1845.

[2] A. D. McKillop, *A Victorian Faust* (Publications of the Modern Language Association of America (1925), XL, 762).

[3] Hallam Lord Tennyson, *Alfred Lord Tennyson, a Memoir*, (1897), I, 234.

[4] Charles Tennyson, *Alfred Tennyson* (1949), 433.

There came a hand between the sun and us
And its five fingers made five nights in air.[1]

Longfellow noted in his Journal, 'T. read us the wonderful
book, *Festus*. For a youth of twenty to write this is a miracle.
The figurative language is magnificent.'[2] Dante Gabriel Rossetti
read it and re-read it with enthusiasm.[3] Matthew Arnold
reckoned Bailey 'among the most promising English verse-
writers'.[4] Walter Savage Landor wrote a kindly Epistle to the
Author of *Festus*, in which he praised the poem and gave the
poet some good advice — and never was advice so unheeded.

Thought erases thought,
As numerous sheep erase each other's print
When spungy moss they press or sterile sand.[5]

Browning greatly admired the poem.

Philip James Bailey had been born at Nottingham in April
1816, the son of the editor and proprietor of the *Nottingham
Mercury*. His father was spoken of as an 'inveterate rhymster';
when his son was ten years old he gave him a copy of *Childe
Harold*, which he learnt by heart, and took him to see
Byron lying in state at the Blackamoor's Head in Nottingham.
Philip James went to Glasgow University at the age of sixteen,
but left after a year and in 1833 began to read for the Bar in
London. He was called in 1840, but never practised. In 1836
he retired to his father's house and began to write a poem. He
already had the plan worked out. It was to be, he told his
father, 'a dramatic poem (if that may be termed dramatic
which boasts no plot, no action; and only a few characters) on a
scheme almost the reverse of that of the Devil and Doctor

[1] *Ibid.*, 215–16.

[2] *Life of Henry Wadsworth Longfellow*, ed. Samuel Longfellow (Boston, 1891), II, 24, quoted in A. D. McKillop, *op. cit.*, 763.

[3] *Dante Gabriel Rossetti: His Family-Letters*, ed. W. M. Rossetti
(1895), I, 89.

[4] *Letters of Matthew Arnold to Arthur Hugh Clough*, ed. H. F. Lowry
(Oxford, 1932), 66 (February 1848).

[5] *The Works and Life of Walter Savage Landor* (1876), VIII,
237–40.

Faustus.'[1] (This, I should add, is not an altogether satisfactory description of the subject.) He finished it in two years.

The rest of his life will not detain us long. He wrote more poetry. He never returned to London. In 1864 he settled for a time in Jersey and often visited the Continent. He came back to England in 1876 and lived in turn near Ilfracombe, at Blackheath and at Nottingham. His first marriage was an unhappy one and he divorced his wife. He married again shortly before going to Jersey. In his old age he seems to have become portentously venerable, 'handsome, almost absurdly, almost irritatingly so, like a picture of Connal, "first of mortal men" in some illustrated edition of Ossian,'[2] as Edmund Gosse put it. He died at the age of eighty-six in September 1902.

But, if Bailey's life was uneventful, it is difficult to imagine that any other poem has had such an extraordinary career, if I may put it that way, as *Festus*. First published in 1839, it went through eleven editions in this country, the last in 1901.[3] There were seven versions. Beginning as a poem of a little over 8000 lines, it eventually grew to be one of just under 40,000. Each new version had revisions, some excision, and a very great many additions.[4] But this was not all that Bailey wrote. Other poems appeared, *The Angel World* in 1850, *The Mystic* in 1855, *The Age; a Colloquial Satire* in 1858; *The Universal Hymn* in 1867. Each was an unqualified failure. Bailey, however, found the way to defeat his public. The popularity of *Festus* remained unaffected; it was even greater in America

---

[1] Philip James Bailey to Thomas Bailey, 26 April, 1836, quoted in A. D. McKillop, *op. cit.*, 744. (This article quotes several of Bailey's letters to his father, some published in the *Christian Science Monitor* in 1910, other unpublished.)

[2] Edmund Gosse, 'Philip James Bailey', *The Fortnightly Review*, 1 November, 1902, 760; reprinted in his *Portraits and Sketches* (1912).

[3] The English editions are listed in Morse Peckham, 'English Editions of Philip James Bailey's Festus'. *Papers of the Bibliographical Society of America*, 1950, XLIV, 55–8. The fifth version, 1860, had six lines fewer than the fourth, 1852.

[4] In the last edition the final third of the poem is largely rewritten, though most of what was in the earlier versions is included.

than in England. There were about thirty pirated editions in
that country in the nineteenth century; a Boston publisher
said in 1855 that he had sold over 22,000 copies.[1] Bailey took
to incorporating large portions of his unsuccessful works,
sometimes almost the whole book, in each new edition of *Festus*.
As a part of *Festus* the poems, which had been ignored on their
own, were accepted without question.

It is difficult to know how to deal with a poem which went
through such an extraordinary development. Most of the critics
who had admired it in its early days held that Bailey eventually
made it unreadable. One might agree, except that it went on
being read. It became in its later stages less lyrical, more
didactic and a great deal more Miltonic. As a work to be studied
or criticised it became quite unmanageable. But to confine one's
attention to the first edition, though a much easier task, would
mean ignoring altogether a most unusual literary phenomenon.
I have based my own study on the second edition of 1845, the
version which some of the greatest poets of his day applauded.

It was to be, he said, 'a dramatic poem which boasts no plot,
no action.' This goes rather too far. It has a plot of a kind and
I do not believe that the poem can be understood without
considering it. But it is an extremely difficult story to tell. I
have read several critical studies of the poem which have
started to tell it, but not one has ever finished it. I shall do so.
I think it is likely that you will be the first audience which has
ever heard the whole plot of Bailey's *Festus*.

The poem in its second edition is divided into thirty-six
scenes, such as Heaven, Hell, Space, Wood and Water —
Sunset, Alcove and Garden, Colonnade and Lawn, A Village
Feast — Evening, A large Party and Entertainment, Another
and a better World, Anywhere, Everywhere and Elsewhere.
(By the tenth edition, that is the seventh version, the number
of scenes had increased to fifty-one and they are a great deal
longer.) The opening, obviously modelled on the *Prolog in
Himmel* of Goethe's *Faust*, is in Heaven. The Seraphim and
Cherubim sing the praises of God, and Lucifer speaks. At once

---

[1] A. D. McKillop, *op. cit.*, 764.

a difference between the two poems is apparent. Mephistopheles speaks for twenty lines and one then knows exactly
with whom one is dealing. Lucifer speaks for more than twice
as long and in what he says he is quite indistinguishable from
the other angels in Heaven.

> Father of spirit, as the sun of air!
> Beginning of all ends, and end of all
> Beginnings, throughout all Eternity;
> From whom Eternity and every power
> Perfect, and pure cause, is and emanates!
> Originator without origin!
> End without end! Creator of all ages,
> And sabbath of all Being; who hast made
> All numbers sacred, who art all and one!

Eventually Lucifer comes to the point,

> Behold I bow before Thee; hear Thou me!
> *God:* What wouldst thou, Lucifer?
> *Lucifer:*   There is a youth
> Among the sons of men I fain would have
> Given up wholly to me.
> *God:*   He is thine,
> To tempt.
> *Lucifer:*   I thank Thee, Lord!
> *God:*   Upon his soul
> Thou hast no power. All souls are mine for aye.
> And I do give thee leave to this that he
> May know my love is more than all his sin,
> And prove unto himself that nought but God
> Can satisfy the soul He maketh great.[1]

God, *der Herr*, in Goethe's poem makes it pretty clear that
Mephistopheles will not be successful in the end, but he does
not go as far as this. As a drama *Festus* collapses in the opening
scene. But Bailey's theology made this inevitable.

---

[1] *Festus: A Poem by Philip James Bailey Barrister at Law*, Second
Edition (London, William Pickering, 1845), 3–4.

He defined the purpose of his poem in a Proem and elaborated this in a Preface to the Jubilee edition of 1889.[1] *Festus* was to proclaim the doctrine of Universalism, the belief that all men would be saved. And, in Bailey's view, there was good reason for this.

> All creatures being faulty by their nature,
> And by God made all liable to sin,
> God only could atone — and unto none
> Except Himself — for universal sin.
> It is thus that God did sacrifice to God,
> Himself unto Himself, in the great way
> Of Triune mystery.

In fact, he says,

> God doth suffer for the sins of those
> Whom he hath made, that are liable to sin.[2]

The Redemption, in this way, comes to be God redeeming Himself and putting right what He Himself has done. It follows, of course, that

> They are forgiven from the first,
>   They are predestined Thine;
> And though in sin they were the worst,
>   In Thee they are divine. . . .
> There is but one great right and good; and ill
> And wrong are shades thereof, not substances.
> Nothing can be antagonist to God.[3]

The Holy Ghost, who has a speaking part, makes Festus's own future assured.

> And I will hallow him to the ends of Heaven,
> That though he plunge his soul in sin like a sword
> In water, it shall nowise cling to him.[4]

[1] The original Proem was abandoned after the second edition and much of it was incorporated in the poem itself. A new Proem appeared in the Jubilee edition.

[2] *Festus*, ix–x.   [3] *Ibid.*, xii.   [4] *Ibid.*, 5.

(Even Miss Elizabeth Barrett admitted that in the poem there was 'some overdaring in relation to divine things, the locutor ship of the Holy Ghost being among them'.[1]) And so, as Lucifer himself says later in the poem,

> Sin, the dead branch upon the tree of Life,
> Shall be cut off for ever; and all souls
> Concluded in God's boundless amnesty.[2]

'There is nothing offensive in it, nothing cainish,' Bailey had assured his father when he was beginning to write the poem.[3] I should say that *Festus* is very cainish indeed. Universalism was no new belief, but I suspect that Bailey found the idea that evil was something for which God must accept responsibility in a dialogue in Byron's drama.

> *Lucifer* [referring to Jehovah and himself]: We *both* reign
> *Cain:* But one of you makes evil.
> *Lucifer:*   Which?
> *Cain:*   Thou! for
> If you canst do man good, why dost thou not?
> *Lucifer:* And why not he who made? *I* made ye not;
> Ye are *his* creatures, and not mine.[4]

The style and poetic diction of *Festus* are obviously derived from Byron's dramatic poems. These do not seem very exciting to us now. They remained so longer in Germany than here. I remember how astonished I was a few years ago to be told by an elderly and very respectable German civil servant that he had been taken as a boy of sixteen to see Byron's *Manfred* and as a result had been in such a state of feverish excitement for three days that he had had to be kept in bed. No doubt Bailey and many other young men of his day were as excited by it. It must be admitted that Byron's *Manfred* and his *Cain* gave Bailey some excuse for the style of his verse.

[1] *Letters of Elizabeth Barrett Browning to Richard Hengist Horne*, ed. S. R. Townshend Mayer (1877), II, 14.

[2] *Festus*, 63.

[3] Letter to Thomas Bailey, 26 April, 1836. Quoted in A. D. McKillop, *op. cit.*, 753.

[4] *Cain, A Mystery*, II, ii.

The poem, however, had another purpose besides that of
showing a man tempted to sin with the absolute certainty of
being covered by an eventual amnesty. In his Proem Bailey
says that he will write of Youth,

> The foibles, follies, trials, sufferings —
> And manifest and manifold are they —
> Of a young, hot, unworld-schooled heart that has
> Had its own way in life, and wherein all
> May see some likeness of their own, — 'tis these
> Attract, unite, and, sunlike, concentrate
> The ever-moving system of our feelings.[1]

Later Festus describes a poem written by a friend, which is
obviously meant to be Bailey's poem itself.

> Thus have I shown the meaning of the book,
> And the most truthful likeness of a mind,
> Which hath as yet been limned: the mind of youth
> In strength and failings, in its overcomings,
> And in its short comings; the kingly ends,
> The universalizing heart of youth;
> Its love of power, heed not how had, although
> With surety of self-ruin at the end.[2]

Bailey, in fact, was more influenced by Byron than by Goethe,
and Festus is frequently a very Byronic young man.

In the next scene, Wood and Water — Sunset, Lucifer comes
to Festus. It is not at all easy to understand exactly with what
Lucifer tempts him, and in the end no particular pact seems to
be made, nor is any time limit set. Lucifer says:

> I came
> And come to proffer thee the earth; to set
> Thee on a throne — the throne of will unbound — [3]

and

> All secrets thou shalt ken — all mysteries construe;
> At nothing marvel. All the veins which stretch,

---

[1] *Festus*, ix.   [2] *Ibid.*, 261.   [3] *Ibid.*, 19.

> Unsearchable by human eyes, of lore
> Most precious, most profound, to thine shall bare
> And vulgar lie like dust,[1]

but he hardly keeps his promises. It is only at the very end of
the poem that Festus becomes King of the Earth, and throughout the poem he is attempting without much success to construe
mysteries, though he is certainly shown a great many.
Lucifer's position, however, is from the start an impossible one.

> *Lucifer:* From God I come.
> *Festus:*   I do believe thee, spirit.
>   He will not let thee harm me. Him I love,
>   And thee I fear not. I obey Him.
> *Lucifer:*   Good.
>   Both time and case are urgent. Come away![2]

As will be seen, however, it is more significant that Lucifer also
says,

> Thou shalt love ten as others love but one.[3]

Festus asks for a 'breathing-space' and the two meet again
at midnight.

> *Lucifer:*   I have command over spirits,
>   Whom wilt thou that I call?
> *Festus:*   Mine Angela!
> *Lucifer:* There is an Angel ever by thine hand.
>   What seest thou?
> *Festus:*   It is my love! It is she!
>   My glory! spirit! beauty, let me touch thee.[4]

Angela soon vanishes and Festus implores Lucifer to call her
again. He proves, however, something of a disappointment.

> I call on spirits and I make them come:
> But they depart according to their own will.[5]

Angela is a girl whom Festus had loved. He had deserted her
and she had died. She will appear again, as Lucifer promises.

[1] *Festus*, 22.   [2] *Ibid.*, 23.   [3] *Ibid.*, 21.
[4] *Ibid.*, 30.   [5] *Ibid.*, 31.

Two scenes later, Alcove and Garden, we find Festus with another lady, Clara, with whom he is now in love. In the end she is to be about as near the *Ewiges weibliches* as the poem ever attains. Her attitude is comparatively straightforward and orthodox.

> True bliss is to be found in holy life;
> In charity to man — in love to God. . . .
> I cannot sing the lightsome lays of love.
> Many thou know'st who can; but none that can
> Love thee as I do — for I love thy soul;
> And I would save it, Festus![1]

With her, Festus, no doubt to make an effective contrast, becomes rather more like a damned soul.

Festus: Nay, I love Death.
  But Immortality, with finger spired,
  Points to a distant, giant world — and says
  There, there is my home! Live along with me!
Clara: Canst see that world?
Festus: Just — a huge shadowy shape;
  It loooks like a disembodied orb — the ghost
  Of some great sphere which God hath stricken dead:
  Or like a world which God hath thought — not made.
Clara: Follow her, Festus! Does she speak again?
Festus: She never speaks but once: and now, in scorn,
  Points to this dim, dwarfed, misbegotten sphere.
Clara: Why let it pass?
Festus: That is the great world-question.[2]

A scene in a Market-place is more interesting and certainly shows some recollections of Goethe's *Faust*. Festus and Lucifer discuss the meaning of Life and Festus expresses some elevating thoughts.

> Life's more than breath and the quick round of blood:
> It is a great spirit and a busy heart.
> The coward and the small in soul scarce do live.

[1] *Festus*, 51–2.   [2] *Ibid.*, 56.

One generous feeling — one great thought — one deed
Of good, ere night, would make life longer seem
Than if each year might number a thousand days, —
Spent as is this by nations of mankind.
We live in deeds, not years; in thoughts, not breaths;
In feelings, not in fingers on a dial.
We should count time by heart-throbs. He most lives
Who thinks most — feels the noblest — acts the best.[1]

These lines were to suffer an appalling fate. They were chosen by I. A. Richards as the first poem to be considered by his pupils, whose comments were published in his *Practical Criticism*. I wonder what Bailey would have thought of the note, 'Appeals to me because it *sums up my creed* as a Socialist, *of service not self*.' I think he would have been pleased. There is a good deal in the poem of what was soon afterwards to be spoken of as Christian Socialism. Of all the criticisms of Bailey's style — and it called forth some very strange ones — none seems to me so surprising as that of one of Richards's group of undergraduates, 'Topping condensation of language.'[2]

To return to the Market-place. A funeral passes and Festus realises that it is Angela's. He gazes on her dead body and speaks of his love for her. Lucifer preaches a sermon outside a church, a kind of parody of a rabidly evangelical address, which makes him for a moment resemble Mephistopheles more closely. This is followed immediately by a very long prayer, nearly 250 lines, delivered by Festus, one of the additions in the second edition. Though very diffuse and repetitive, it is impressive, mainly because Bailey for once abandons almost entirely the attempt to be 'poetic' and writes in an unadorned style. Yet he does succeed in giving what I can only call a liturgical impression. In spite of some absurdities, it is the most interesting passage in the poem. If I had to compile an anthology to illustrate the political and social thought of the Victorian era I should include the whole prayer. As we read

---

[1] *Festus*, 64.

[2] I. A. Richards, *Practical Criticism: A Study in Literary Judgment* (1929), 20–30.

it we recognise that here, in a primitive form, are a good many
of the ideas of our own day, even some of those which we believe
our own century may claim credit for.

> Peace, there my friends! one minute; let us pray!
> Grant us, oh God! that in Thy holy love
> The universal people of the world
> May grow more great and happy every day;
> Mightier, wiser, humbler, too, towards Thee.
> And that all ranks, all classes, callings, states
> Of life, so far as such seem right to Thee,
> May mingle into one, like sister trees,
> And so in one stem flourish. . . .

There is a strange passage on the relationship between king
and people, the most bizarre expression of the doctrine of the
Social Contract I have ever met with. This is followed by one
which deals with what may seem to be a more pressing problem,
that of the demands made on the people when their sovereignty
is granted them. We should remember, however, that these
lines were written before 1848.

> Let both remember, Lord!
> They are but things like-natured with all nations;
> That mountains issue out of plains, and not
> Plains out of mountains, and so likewise kings
> Are of the people, not the people of kings. . . .
> > Grant
> That nations may now ooo, it is not kings,
> Nor priests they need fear so much as themselves;
> That if they keep but true to themselves, and free,
> Sober, enlightened, godly — mortal men
> Become impassable as air, one great
> And indestructible substance as the sea. . . .

One passage deals with change and progress.

> The bells of time are ringing changes fast.
> Grant, Lord! that each fresh peal may usher in
> An era of advancement, that each change
> Prove an effectual, lasting, happy gain.
> And we beseech Thee, overrule, oh God!

> All civil contests to the good of all;
> All party and religious difference
> To honourable ends. . . .

He considers with satisfaction the prospect of higher living-standards and the spread of education and in one remarkable passage speaks of the effects of industrialisation, — one might almost say of automation.

> Grant us, All-maintaining Sire!
> That all the great mechanic aids to toil
> Man's skill hath formed, found, rendered — whether used
> In multiplying works of mind, or aught
> To obviate the thousand wants of life,
> May much avail to human welfare now
> And in all ages, henceforth and for ever!
> Let their effect be, Lord! to lighten labour,
> And give more room to mind, and leave the poor
> Some time for self-improvement. . . .

In a very interesting passage he raises the question of his own nation's imperial destiny,

> Vouchsafe, kind God! Thy blessing to this isle,
> Specially! May our country ever lead
> The world, for she is worthiest; and may all
> Profit by her example, and adopt
> Her course, wherever great, or free, or just.
> May all her subject colonies and powers
> Have of her freedom freely, as a child
> Receiveth of its parents. Let not rights
> Be wrested from us to our own reproach,
> But granted. . . .

A consideration of British foreign policy may help us to understand the bellicosity to be found in some of Tennyson's poems of this period, which disturbed at the time — and disturbs now — some of his admirers.

> If policy or self-defence call forth
> Our forces to the field, let us in Thee
> Place, first, our trust, and in Thy name we shall
> O'ercome, for we will only wage the right . . .

> Till then, Lord God of armies, let our foes
> Have their swords broken and their cannon burst,
> And their strong cities levelled; and while we
> Ware faithfully and righteously, improve,
> Civilize, christianize the lands we win
> From savage or from nature, Thou, oh God!
> Wilt aid and hallow conquest, as of old,
> Thine own immediate nation's.

He looks forward, however, to the day when 'all mankind may make one brotherhood', and

> every race
> Red, black or white, olive, or tawny-skinned,
> Settle in peace and swell the gathering hosts
> Of the great Prince of Peace!

The prayer ends,

> For the one true faith we pray;
> There is but one in Heaven and there shall be
> But one on earth, the same which is in Heaven.
> Prophecy is more true than history.
> Grant us our prayers, we pray, Lord! in the name
> And for the sake of Thy Son Jesus Christ,
> Our Saviour and Redeemer, who with Thee,
> And with the Holy Spirit, reigneth God
> Over all worlds, one blessed Trinity![1]

The highly orthodox doxology is surprising. It was to last until the seventh edition, but eventually disappeared.

> The bells of time are ringing changes fast.
> Grant, Lord, that each fresh peal may usher in
> An era of advancement.

It is interesting to speculate whether Tennyson was influenced by this prayer when he wrote the famous stanzas in *In Memoriam*,

> Ring out, wild bells, to the wild sky.[2]

---

[1] *Festus*, 75–82.

[2] The question is discussed shortly in H. N. Fairchild, 'Wild Bells in Bailey's Festus?', *Modern Language Notes* (1949), LXIV, 256–8.

Most of the aspirations in Tennyson's verses are to be found in
Bailey's poem and there are several verbal coincidences.
Tennyson probably wrote them soon after he had read *Festus*.
There are certainly some Festian echoes in the introductory
poem to *In Memoriam*, written in 1849.

In the next scene, styled The Surface, Lucifer and Festus
ride on winged horses over the earth, looking down on the
countries below them, such as Tartar land, Hindustan, Afric's
plain,

> America! half-brother of the world!
> With something good and bad of every land,[1]

and finally England. Bailey omitted in his second edition the
picture in the original version of the English people on their
knees before 'a maiden fair', singing, 'Hail, Victoria! Princess,
hail!' This scene has some dashing lines and Bailey perhaps
had the Walpurgisnacht in mind.

> Come hither, come hither,
> My brave black steed!
> And thou, too, its fellow,
> Hither with speed!
> Though not so fleet
> As the steeds of Death,
> Your feet are as sure,
> Ye have longer breath.
> Ye have drawn the world
> Without wind or bait,
> Six thousand years,
> And it waxeth late;
> So take me this once,
> And again to my home,
> And rest ye and feast ye.
> They come, they come.[2]

These lines were omitted in the final version, no doubt as not
being sufficiently dignified. On the other hand the ride over

---

[1] *Festus*, 94.   [2] *Ibid.*, 85.

the earth was made a great deal more geographically all-embracing.

In the next scene, A Village Feast — Evening, we have three of the songs which Bailey introduces fairly frequently in the poem. 'My gipsy maid! my gipsy maid!' seems to me a very tepid performance, though I must admit that Edmund Gosse thought it 'a vivid improvisation as we could imagine a bard composing by a watch-fire in a mountain-pass'. One of the songs is interesting as an early example of the influence of Robert Burns on English poetry. The result could hardly be more deplorable.

> Oh! the wee green neuk, the sly green neuk,
>   The wee sly neuk for me!
> Whare the wheat is wavin' bright and brown,
>   And the wind is fresh and free.
> Whare I weave wild weeds, and out o' reeds
>   Kerve whissles as I lay;
> And a douce low voice is murmurin' by
>   Through the lee-lang simmer day.
>   Oh! the wee green neuk, &c.[1]

In this scene we meet for the first time a Student, who makes several more appearances. At first he is a recognisable character with a recognisable point of view.

> When night hath set her silver lamp on high,
> Then is the time for study; when Heaven's light
> Pours itself on the page, like prophecy
> On time, unglooming all its mighty meanings;
> It is then we feel the sweet strength of the stars,
> And magic of the moon.

Lucifer, who has his more saturnine moments, comments,

> It's a bad habit.[2]

But Bailey could never maintain a character, and before long the Student and Festus speak almost the same language.

I should explain that, as the scenes succeed one another,

[1] *Festus*, 103.   [2] *Ibid.*, 106.

almost everything imaginable is discussed. Some lines or
phrases, here and there, stand out, such as one from one of the
more melancholy of Festus's speeches.

> We leave
> Our home in youth — no matter to what end; —
> Study — or strife — or pleasure, or what not;
> And coming back in few short years, we find
> All as we left it, outside; the old elms,
> The house, grass, gates, and latchet's selfsame click:
> But lift that latchet, — all is changed as doom:
> The servants have forgotten our step, and more
> Than half of those who knew us know us not.[1]

It would hardly be fair to say that, if one writes a poem of
over 13,000 lines, a few must be successful. Bailey should be
given credit for the 'latchet's selfsame click'. But 'all is changed
as doom' is quite meaningless; he is merely using grand words.
One has to be ready for a great deal of that.

At the end of a scene, called A Metropolis — a Public Place,
Lucifer makes Festus 'recline calmly on yon marble slab as
though asleep'. He puts him into a trance and they visit, first,
The Air, and then Another and a better World, which turns
out to be the planet Venus. There Festus meets not only his
Muse, but also Angela once more. He declares,

> When I forget that the stars shine in air —
> When I forget that beauty is in stars —
> When I forget that love with beauty is —
> Will I forget thee.[2]

When, not long before, he had met Clara in the Alcove and
Garden, he had said,

> Thou art my first, last, only love; nor shall
> Another even tempt my heart.[3]

However, the next scene after the one on the planet, styled A
large Party and Entertainment — Festus, Ladies, and Others,
begins,

[1] *Ibid.*, 98.   [2] *Ibid.*, 157.   [3] *Ibid.*, 53.

Festus: My Helen! let us rest awhile,
   For most I love thy calmer smile;
   We'll not be missed from this gay throng,
   They dance so eagerly and long,

and very soon he makes his feelings perfectly clear.

   I love thee, and will leave thee never,
   Until my soul leave life for ever.[1]

In this scene we are made to realise fully that the poem is one about contemporary life. The names of those at the party can leave us in no doubt: Will, Charles, Laurence, Henry, Frederic, Frank, Walter, George, Edward, Fanny, Emma, Lucy and Marian. Festus has a speech to Helen comparing her to wine,

   Thy nature is so pure and fine,
   'Tis most like wine;
   Thy blood, which blushes through each vein,
   Rosy champagne;
   And the fair skin which o'er it grows,
   Bright as its snows.
   Thy wit, which thou dost work so well,
   Is like cool moselle;
   Like madeira, bright and warm,
   Is thy smile's charm;
   Claret's glory hath thine eye,
   Or mine must lie;
   But nought can like thy lips possess
   Deliciousness;
   And now that thou'rt divinely merry,
   I'll kiss and call thee sparkling sherry.[2]

Any social historian could deduce in a moment when, and when alone, this particular list of wines could have been drawn up to describe a mistress. The scene ends with words which also anchor it to its period.

George: How goes the enemy?
Lucifer: What can he mean?
Festus: He ask the hour.

[1] *Festus*, 159–60.   [2] *Ibid.*, 160.

Lucifer (who undoubtedly has his moments): Aha! then **I**
    Advise, if Time thy foe hath been,
    Be quick! shake hands, man, with Eternity.[1]

At one point it is divulged that Festus has had an affair with
Marian and has deserted her. Helen is now his mistress. But
he does not fail to be Byronic. He sings a song to the beautiful
maidens of different countries, ending,

> Here's to beauty, young beauty, all over the world!
> *Will:* Hurrah! a glorious toast;
>   'Twould warm a ghost.
> *Festus:* It moves not me. I cannot drink
>   The toast I have given.
>   There! — Earth may pledge it, and she will —
>   Herself and her beauty to Heaven.
>   Drink to the dead — youth's feelings vain!
>   Drink to the heart — the battered wreck,
>   Hurled from all passion's stormy main![2]

On the whole the dialogue in this scene moves unusually
quickly, though Helen at one point apostrophises the moon for
over sixty lines and Festus has an even longer soliloquy 'apart',
in which he remembers Angela and asks for forgiveness. This
is the only occasion in the poem when he recalls one lady in the
presence of another, and the only time that Bailey attempts to
place Festus's relationships with women in the framework of his
sins and eventual forgiveness.

> Thou wilt forgive, if once with thee
> I limned the outline of a Heaven;
> But go and tell our God, from me,
> He must forgive what He hath given;
> And, if we be by passion driven
> To love, and all its natural madness,
> Tell Him, that man by love hath thriven,
> And that by love he shall be shriven;
> For God is love, where love is gladness.

Although much of the diction is very weak, the whole speech is,
I feel, better than most in the poem. It is certainly the least

[1] *Festus*, 192.   [2] *Ibid.*, 191.

undisciplined. It is built up on a kind of refrain. I can show this
by taking a few lines, omitting a good many.

> Oh! can it — can it be forgiven,
> That I forget thou art in Heaven?
> Thou wilt forgive me this, and more:
> Love spends his all, and still hath store.
> Thou wilt forgive, if beauty's wile
> Should win, perforce, one glance from me;
> When they, whose art it is to smile,
> Can never smile my heart from thee . . .
> Thou wilt forgive, if now and then
> I link with hands less loved than thine . . .
> Thou wilt forgive me, if my feet
> Should move to music with the fair;
> When at each turn, I burn to meet
> Thy stream-like step and aëry air . . .
> Thou wilt forgive, if e'er my heart
> Err from the orbit of its love . . .
> Thou wilt forgive, if soft white arms
> Embrace, by fits, this breast of mine.[1]

For once Bailey seems to me able to control the rhythm of his
verse. It may give some idea of what happened to the poem
eventually if I note that in the final version Helen and Marian
have to listen to a speech by Festus of 1994 lines.[2]

There follow scenes in a Church-yard, Space, and even in
Heaven, where Festus meets God for a brief moment, and also
his Genius and Guardian Angel. It is impossible to give a just
impression of the long discourses and discussions here and
throughout the poem. Occasionally Bailey is buoyed up by the
Bible and Milton.

> Listen! I hear the harmonies of Heaven,
> From sphere to sphere and from the boundless round
> Re-echoing bliss to those serenest heights

---

[1] *Festus*, 182–4.

[2] *Festus*, Fiftieth-Anniversary Edition (1893), 281–319. Helen
receives this speech with the startling reply of a single line,

> Silence may be best speaks experience.

Where angels sit and strike their emulous harps,
Wreathed round with flowers and diamonded with dew;
Such dew as gemmed the everduring blooms
Of Eden winterless, or as all night
The tree of Life wept from its every leaf
Unwithering. And now methinks I hear
The music of the murmur of the stream
Which through the Bridal City of the Lord
Floweth all life for ever; and the breath
Through the star-shading branches of that Tree
Transplanted now to Heaven, but once on earth,
Whose fruit is for all Beings — breathed of God.
Oh! breathe on me, inspiring spirit-breath!
Oh! flow to me, ye heart-reviving waves;
Freshen the faded soul that droops and dies.[1]

It is often difficult to tell whether Festus is speaking what
Bailey considered to be heresy or orthodoxy. But this fragment
will show what to Bailey was unimpeachably orthodox.

The soul is but an organ, and it hath
No power of good or evil in itself,
More than the eye hath power of light or dark.
God fitted it for good; and evil is
Good in another way we are not skilled in.
The good we do is of His own good will, —
The ill of His own letting . . .
Yet merit or demerit none I see
In nature, human or material,
In passions or affections good or bad.
We only know that God's best purposes
Are oftenest brought about by dreadest sins.
Is thunder evil or is dew divine?
Does virtue lie in sunshine, sin in storm?
Is not each natural, each needful, best?
How know we what is evil from what good?
Wrath and revenge God claimeth as His own.
And yet men speculate on right and wrong

[1] *Festus*, 193–4.

As upon day and night, forgetting both
Have but one cause, and that the same — God's will,
Originally, ultimately, Him . . .

The Angel, with whom he is speaking, (they are in Heaven) —
it is, in fact, his Mother — can only answer,

There lacks in souls like thine unsaved, unraised,
The light within — the light of perfectness —
Such as there is in Heaven. The soul hath sunk
And perished like a light-house in the sea;
It is for God to raise it and rebuild,

and his Genius can only add,

And his, thy son's, He will raise.[1]

Two long scenes give us Festus and Helen passionately in
love and carrying on endless discussions. There is a moment
in the first which shows what Bailey might have made of Lucifer,
if he had not felt bound to give him such a very great deal
to talk about. Festus is telling Helen in most rhapsodical verse
of some of the mysterious beings whom he meets in Space and
one of them he describes at great length,

The spirit evil of the universe,
Impersonate.

Lucifer suddenly enters,

Dost recognize
The portrait, lady?
Helen: Festus! who is this?
What portrait? —
Festus: Wherefore com'st thou? Did I not
Claim privacy one evening?

[1] *Festus*, 202–4. In later editions, e.g. Seventh Edition, Enlarged
(1864), pp. 218–56, there comes next a long scene, A Garden and
Pleasure House, in which Festus is absent. We meet there those who
were present at the party, with some new characters, Sophia, Laura
and Caroline. Frederic tells a Ghost Story — in fourteeners. Laurence
is hopelessly in love with Marian, but she has given her heart to
Festus.

Lucifer: Why, indeed —
I simply called, as I was on my way
To Jupiter — and he's a mouthful, mind; —
To keep the proverbs, too, in countenance.
Any commands for our planetary friends?
I go. Make my excuses!   [*Goes.*]
Festus: A mistake,
Dearest; but rectified.[1]

And he proceeds to describe in 160 lines another Angel. Some
lines in this passage will show how utterly incapable Bailey
was of letting well alone.

'Twas on a lovely summer afternoon,
Close by the grassy marge of a deep tarn,
Nigh halfway up a mountain, that we stood,
I and the angel, when she told me this.
Above us rose the grey rocks, by our side
Forests of pines, and the bright breaking wavelets
Came crowding, dancing to the brink, like thoughts
Unto our lips. Before us shone the sun.
The angel waved her hand ere she began,
As bidding earth be still. The birds ceased singing
And the trees breathing, and the lake smoothed down
Each shining wrinkle, and the wind drew off.
Time leant him o'er his scythe and, listening, wept.
The circling world reined in her lightning pace
A moment; Ocean hushed his snow-maned steeds,
And a cloud hid the sun, as doth the face
A meditative hand: then spake she thus: — [2]

In the second scene, where Helen is at her piano, the Student
intervenes. His sentiments and speech have now become
indistinguishable from Festus's. It contains a long account of
a young friend of Festus and a book he wrote; Bailey, I feel,
is thinking of both Byron and himself. Although it is almost
interminable and interrupted with long passages which lead us
far from the theme — well over a thousand lines in all — there
is a sincerity in this scene to be found hardly anywhere else in

[1] *Festus*, 218–19.   [2] *Ibid.*, 220–1.

the poem. The ending is quite dramatic and, if one forgets the poems which the public refused to read, strangely prophetic of the author's future.

Student: Say, did thy friend
    Write aught beside the work thou tell'st of?
Festus: Nothing.
    After that, like the burning peak, he fell
    Into himself, and was missing ever after.
Student: If not a secret, pray who was he?
Festus: I.[1]

The next scene, Garden and Bower by the Sea, is indeed surprising. Lucifer now falls in love. The lady, Elissa, who has not appeared before,[2] is at times a little more individualised than the others. Lucifer, to her intense grief, has to leave her, though he promises to return.

Elissa: But when wilt thou come back?
Lucifer: Almost before thou wishest. He will know.
    [He is referring to Festus who has joined them.]
Elissa: I shall be always asking him. Farewell.   (*She goes.*)
Lucifer: Shine on, ye stars! and light her to her rest;
    Scarce are ye worthy for her handmaidens.
    Why, Hell would laugh to learn I had been in love.
    I have affairs in Hell. Wilt go with me?
Festus: Yes, in a month or two: — not just this minute.
Lucifer: I shall be there and back again ere then.
Festus: Meanwhile I can amuse myself: so, go!
    But sometime I would fain behold thy home,
    And pass the gates of fire.
Lucifer: And so thou shalt.
    My home is everywhere where spirit is.
    All things are as I meant them. Fare thee well.   (*He goes.*)

[1] *Festus*, 273.

[2] In later editions Elissa appears for a short time, along with Clara and Helen, accompanying the bier of Angela in the scene in the Market-place. Later, when Lucifer breaks in on Festus and Helen, and is given a great deal more to say, he describes 'a form of queenly beauty', whom he had seen 'seated by the sea'. Helen recognizes her as Elissa, with whom she had ceased to be friendly.

> *Festus:* The strongest passion which I have is honour:
> I would I had none: it is in my way.[1]

It is obvious enough what is going to happen, but it does not happen at once. There are four scenes to come first, Everywhere, in which Festus and Lucifer discourse of many things, such as Eternity and the mind of God; Hell, where they have a long discussion with the Son of God, who rescues a Fiend; Colonnade and Lawn, in which Festus meets Clara again and tells her something of his experiences; and the Sun in which Festus has a soliloquy of about a hundred lines. Clara always carries with her some reminiscences of Goethe's Margarete,

> O Festus! I conjure thee to beware
> Lest thus the Evil one thy soul ensnare.[2]

And then comes: A Drawing Room, Festus and Elissa.

> *Festus:* Who says he loves and is not wretched, lies . . .
> In the name of God,
> What made us love, Elissa?
> *Elissa:*   I know not.
> I am not happy. I have wept all day.

Elissa, however, is now helplessly in love with Festus,

> Festus! I will, I can love none but thee.

And as for Festus,

> All hours not spent with thee are blanks between stars.
> I love thee! love thee! love thee! madly love thee!
> Oh! thou hast drank my heart dry of all love!
> It will be empty to aught after thee.[3]

A Singer comes in and sings two verses of a song on the fickleness of woman's love.

> *Elissa:* Methinks I must have heard that voice before.
> *Festus:* And I.
> *Elissa:*   Where?
> *Festus:*   I forget.
> *Elissa:*   And so do I.

---

[1] *Festus*, 290–1.   [2] *Ibid.*, 322.
[3] *Ibid.*, 326–8. ('Drank' in subsequent editions also.)

The Singer finishes the song.

> *Festus:* Come hither, man! I wish to look at thee,
> A moment. No! it can't be. Yet I have seen
> Some one much like thee.
> *Elissa:*   It was a brother, may be?
> *Singer:* I have none, lady. Have ye done with me?
> *Festus:* Yes — go!   (*The singer goes out.*)[1]

Elissa is very uneasy at the thought of Lucifer's return. As
Festus makes passionate love to her, Lucifer enters.

>   Friend!
> Did ye not know me? It was I who sang.[2]

There is a long discussion on the difficult situation the three
find themselves in, which ends with Lucifer leaving them.

> *Lucifer:* Now let us part, or I shall die of wrath.
> Be my estrangement perfect as my love!
> *Elissa:* Part then!
> *Lucifer:*   Thank God it is for eternity![3]

But it is not. In the next scene Lucifer returns to her. He now
shows a certain grandeur.

> *Elissa:* And who art thou that I should fear and serve?
> *Lucifer:* I am the morning and the evening star,
> The star thou lovest and thy lover too;
> I am that star! . . .
>   Look at me!
> Am I not more than mortal in my form?
> Millions of years have circled round my brow
> Like worlds upon their centres; — still I live;
> And age but presses with a halo's weight.
> This single arm hath dashed the light of Heaven;
> This one hand dragged the angels from their thrones: —
> Am I not worthy to have loved thee, lady?[4]

At a word from Lucifer, Elissa dies. Festus comes in,

> Fiend! what is this? Elissa! — she is not dead.
> *Lucifer:* She is. I bade her die, as I had reason.

[1] *Festus*, 333–4.   [2] *Ibid.*, 338.   [3] *Ibid.*, 340.   [4] *Ibid.*, 345.

Festus: Now do I hate thee and renounce thee for ever! —
Abhor thee — go!
Lucifer: Who seeks the other first?
I am gone.
Festus: Away, Fiend! Leave me! My Elissa![1]

But Festus needs Lucifer and in the next scene, A Library and
Balcony — A Summer Night, he summons him again. He is
now in despair.

> And if I have enjoyed more love than others,
> It is but superior suffering, and is more
> Than balanced by the loss of one we love.
> And love itself, hath passed. One fond fair girl
> Remains; one only, and she loves me still.
> But it is not love I feel: it is pure kindness.
> How shall I find another like my last?
> The golden and the gorgeous loveliness —

[1] *Festus*, 347. Bailey was not quite comfortable about Festus's
affair with Elissa. In the Seventh Edition, Enlarged (1864), there is
a remarkable Index to the poem, obviously compiled by Bailey
himself. Under the heading, Festus, we read: Manifests a culpable
passion with regard to Elissa, 428–38; but self-conscious of his fault,
gives thanks to his guardian angel for the unexpected intervention of
Lucifer, 438. It is true that Festus, in later editions, declares, on
Lucifer's unexpected return,

> Saved from myself as though against my will,
> Oh what a mountain-cloud rolls from my heart!
> Where art thou, angel-guard, that I may give
> Thee thanks, if due, for life saved from remorse,
> And sin's soul-blinding sophistries?

But the Guardian Angel's intervention (not in the Second Edition) is
a very brief one and a few lines later Festus is saying to Lucifer, just
as he had in the earlier version,

> She loved thee first — then me. What wouldst thou more?
> Thy heart's embrace, though close, was snake-like cold;
> And mine was warm, and what is more was welcome.

In the final version, however, Festus shows deep remorse and it is
his Guardian Angel's part to comfort him.

A sunset beauty! Ah, I saw it set.
My heart, alas! set with it.[1]

The 'one fond fair girl', who still loves him, is Clara. By now he has quite forgotten Angela, and Helen has faded out of the story without any explanation.[2] In later versions Bailey was to extend greatly the part of Clara, who eventually marries Festus. Their brief honeymoon of 2241 lines of discussion is interrupted by the end of the world. In this edition, however, Clara, as we shall see, is to make only a single very short reappearance.

Lucifer now proffers Festus 'the power which thou dost long for'.

Festus: I have had enough of the infinities:
I am moderate now. I will have the throne of earth.[3]

Lucifer warns him that if he is granted his request, the world will end and he must die with it. Festus is ready for this.

Well, then — be it now! I live but for myself —
The whole world but for me. Friends, loves, and all
I sought, abandon me. It is time to die.
I am yet young; yet I have been deserted,
And wronged, by those whom most I have loved and served.
Sun, moon, and stars! May they all fall on me
When next I trust another — man or woman.[4]

Festus is seen throned as King of the Earth. He just hints at the policy of his government,

Let each one labour for the common weal,
and
The world shall rest, and moss itself with peace,[5]

(themes to be greatly elaborated in later editions) when the peoples of the earth are destroyed.

All around me die. The earth is one great death-bed.

---

[1] *Festus*, 351–2.
[2] In later editions Festus meets Angela again in the Sun. Also, in a very obscure narrative, he tells how he had travelled with the Student and Helen in search of 'mount of awe'. The Student was drowned in a torrent, and Helen, as the ground 'slode, crabwise', fell into an abyss and was killed. (Seventh Edition, Enlarged (1864), pp. 423–4; 449–52.)
[3] *Festus*, 354.   [4] *Ibid.*, 355.   [5] *Ibid.*, 366.

At this point Clara appears.

> Oh! save me, Festus! I have fled to thee,
> Through all the countless nations of yon dead . . .
> I knew — I was sure, that I should die by thee.
> The heart is a true oracle — I knew it!
> *Festus:* Then there is faith among these mortals yet.
> Thy beauty cometh first, and goeth last —
> Willow-like. Welcome![1]

Clara dies in his arms and Festus hears the voice of God,

> Man, die![2]

There are still six scenes to come. Festus finds himself first on the Millenial Earth and then in Hades, where 'the mighty nothings man have made' speak, Jove, Bramh, and Boodh.[3] (By the final edition speeches had been added for Apollo, Osiris, Aurmazd and Odin. In the Seventh there were also speeches by Dionysus and, strangely enough, Allah.) Death proclaims, 'The end's at hand.' The Last Judgment is held and then, in the Heaven of Heavens, the Recording Angel declares,

> All men are judged save one.

The Son of God proclaims, 'He too is saved.'[4] That Festus should be saved was inevitable from the beginning. Nor should we be surprised that last of all God says,

> Take Lucifer, thy place. This day art thou
> Redeemed to archangelic state.[5]

And I suppose we should not be surprised at what follows. Festus's Guardian Angel calls him,

> Hither with me!
> *Festus:*   But where are those I love?
> *Angel:* Yon happy troop!
> *Festus:*   Ah, blest ones, come to me!
> Loves of my heart, on earth; and soul, in Heaven!
> Are ye all here, too, with me?

And they answer, 'All.'

> *Festus:* It is Heaven.[6]

---

[1] *Festus*, 368. [2] *Ibid.*, 371. [3] *Ibid.*, 381.
[4] *Ibid.*, 391. [5] *Ibid.*, 394. [6] *Ibid.*, 394.

What am I to say in face of this? Am I right to feel that only by finding it ridiculous can I avoid being shocked? Or is it that Bailey had the moral courage to press his universalist creed to its logical conclusion, and that I should accept Coleridge's demand, willingly suspend my disbelief in it and approve his whole-heartedness? Should I at least extend my tolerance so far as to find in him a pleasing naivety?

Here, I find, is a poem which was admired by poets whom I admire, Landor, Tennyson, Browning and Matthew Arnold, but I can share nothing of their enthusiasm. What was poetry for them is not poetry for me. How could Tennyson have 'silenced criticism' by quoting the lines,

> There came a hand between the sun and us
> And its five fingers made five nights in air?[1]

How could Asquith have written, 'That there are striking lines and even good passages in *Festus* is not to be denied: such, for instance, as the description of genius as:

> A zigzag streak of lightning in the brain?'[2]

The first two lines of the whole poem seem to me effective, the third meaningless,

> Eternity hath snowed its years upon them;
> And the white winter of their age is come,
> The world and all its worlds; and all shall end.

William Michael Rossetti thought them 'sublime'.[3] Oliver Elton is a critic I respect; he claimed, 'Lines and scraps and flashes show that Bailey has poetry in him somewhere: [He quotes from a description of a sunset.]

[1] *Festus*, 286. It is understandable that Tennyson did not quote at a dinner-party the three lines that immediately follow these.

> God tore the glory from the sun's broad brow,
> And flung the flaming scalp off flat to Hell.
> I saw Him do it; and it passed close by us.

[2] Earl of Oxford and Asquith, *Memories and Reflections* (1928), I, 51.
[3] *Dante Gabriel Rossetti: His Family-Letters*, ed. W. M. Rossetti, I, 89.

> The last high upward slant of sun on the trees,
> Like a dead soldier's sword upon the pall,
> Seems to console earth for the glory gone.'[1]

I can appreciate the first line. In fact, while I should agree that there is some vigorous verse in the poem, some of which I have quoted, this seems to me its only line of genuine poetry. But the simile that follows is, to my mind, strained and sentimental. The sharp picture of the first line is diffused by this obvious effort to dramatise the sunset, and its effect is lost.

> The language of feeling [Bailey once wrote] is one simple idea at once and the first word that comes uppermost. And as people in ordinary life do anything but strain after conceits, it will be found that the poets of nature, and of humanity, have ever uttered their most striking and affecting thoughts in the simplest and most ordinary clothing.[2]

(Rather strangely, Bailey called this quality in poetry, 'quaintness'.) I have no doubt that he meant what he said; but it was not what he did in practice.

'The last high upward slant of sun on the trees.' The line will not bear too much examination, but its success is due to the word, 'slant', which produced exactly, no simile being needed, the image which the poet had in mind, and to the slight irregularity in the metre. But this was not enough for Bailey. So he constantly wrote lines such as these, and I cannot believe that they are poetry.

> The lakelet now, no longer vext with gusts,
> Replaces on her breast the pictured moon
> Pearled round with stars.[3]

> The tree tops stir not:
> But stand and peer on Heaven's bright face as though

[1] Oliver Elton, *Survey of English Literature, 1830–1880* (1920), II, 88. *Festus*, 347.

[2] Letter to Thomas Bailey (n.d.), quoted in A. D. McKillop, *op. cit.*, 752.

[3] *Festus*, 23.

It slept and they were loving it.[1]

[God] shook
The stars from Heaven like rain-drops from a bough;
Like tears they poured adown creation's face.[2]

Only too often the nineteenth-century successors of the great
Romantic poets attempted, sometimes with a desperate
earnestness, to make poetry out of 'simple clothing' by means of
far-fetched and surprising similes or metaphors and by a recourse to the pathetic fallacy. One of the great disadvantages
of reading Bailey is that afterwards one is constantly noticing
passages in the great Victorian poets which could be incorporated in *Festus* without questions asked.

Nor was Bailey really faithful to his demand for simple
words. When necessary he was quite prepared to invent new
ones of his own, such as these: 'making itself a lonelihood of
Right', 'in its sublime samesoundingness',

Some of these bodies whom I speak of are
Pure spirits, others bodies soulical,

'sacred seat of intellective time', 'I shall first promulge a few
good rules', 'God, first and last in Threelihood', 'there stood a
gleedlike throne'. 'I am an omnist and believe in all religions'.[3]

It is not difficult to account for the popularity of *Festus*, if
one bears in mind the stamina of the nineteenth-century reader.
The way had been prepared for its style and diction. Its
liberal theology and highmindedness were wholly in accord
with the ideals and tastes of the day. If it had passages which
might be considered shocking, they were hidden from view by
a cloud of noble sentiments. It is more difficult to understand
why it became, not only unread, but unheard of, so suddenly.

If one analyses the reputation of Bailey's *Festus*, one can see
that it passed through three stages. For a time, though not for
very long, it was highly regarded by the leading poets of the day.
It was ignored by their successors, though it remained a very
popular poem. Then it disappeared from view altogether.

[1] *Festus*, 53.   [2] *Ibid.*, 301.
[3] *Ibid.*, 24, 44, 215, 131, 186, 254, 256, 124.

I think the cause of its disappearance from what one might call high literary society may be determined exactly. In May 1854 Blackwood's published a review of *Firmilian: A Tragedy* by T. Percy Jones, which was claimed as a representative of the Spasmodic School. The play itself was published a few months later. It was actually by William Aytoun and it is, in my view, one of the most brilliant parodies in English literature. The review in *Blackwood's*, which was also written by Aytoun, makes it quite clear that he had *Festus* particularly in mind when he wrote his tragedy. In fact, I cannot help thinking that there is at least one good reason for reading *Festus*: one cannot properly appreciate *Firmilian* unless one has done so. I can only allow myself one quotation from the opening to S cene XIV

Scene. A Garden

Firmilian: My Mariana!
Mariana: O my beautiful!
My seraph-love — my panther of the wild —
My moon-eyed leopard — my voluptuous lord!
O, I am sunk within a sea of bliss,
And find no soundings!
Firmilian: Shall I answer back?
As the great Earth lies silent all the night,
And looks with hungry longing on the stars,
Whilst its huge heart beats on its granite ribs
With measured pulsings of delirious joy —
So look I, Mariana, on thine eyes![1]

Festus never recovered its position in the eyes of those with any literary judgment, but it was still to enjoy fifty years of great popularity. And Bailey cannot be disposed of simply as a poet in the same class as, for example, Ella Wheeler Wilcox. After all, he had for a time an impressive team of supporters.

I cannot then avoid the issue. How am I to read this poem? I am not willing to suspend my disbelief. A creed like Bailey's, which rejected with scorn Original Sin and Free Will, and with them all genuine humility and the need for discipline in life, was bound to lead to poetry like *Festus*. That men like Tennyson

[1] William Edmonstone Aytoun, *Poems* (Oxford, 1921), 349.

admired it is evidence of the weakness of the civilisation of the
nineteenth century, evidence, perhaps, of its coming dissolution.

I look back on the six authors and their works which I have
considered. The other five may have seemed absurd to me at
times, and yet, to use Charles Lamb's comment on William
Warner, they have given me pleasure, and sometimes more than
that. Lines or phrases have stayed in the memory and have
been able to excite me even when they have become familiar to
me; longer passages, not well remembered, have left me with a
desire to read them again, knowing that I shall experience
delight and admiration; often I have found myself respecting
their authors. But all these writers have been spoken of by
others as I have spoken of Philip James Bailey, especially by
the generations immediately following their own. He died less
than a year before I was born. Perhaps that explains everything. Few works of literature can survive the period of reaction against them, and unless they do, nearly all will sink without trace. During this period it is little use for the diver to
descend and peer at them through the muddy waters of the
sea's depths, which they stir up as they gently settle on the
bottom. Later, perhaps, he may do so and see a gem here and
there, as he clambers through the ship's hold.

But perhaps he had better not. That was what Valéry said
in one of the most beautiful of his *Variétés*,[1] which has haunted
me with an accusing finger as I have prepared these lectures.
And so, as an act of penitence, it is with his words that I shall
close the last of them.

'The greatest part of what we write is fated to become utterly
insignificant or merely quaint. Successive generations react to
it less and less or consider it more and more as the unsophis-
ticated or inconceivably freakish production of another race of
men. With works that have been materially preserved there
elapses, between the full vigour of their prime and the finality
of death, a period during which they are imperceptibly defaced

[1] Paul Valéry, *Variété II* (Paris, 1930), 50-2, *Oraison funèbre d'une
fable.*

and gradually corrupted. They are sick unto death, though not
at first in their actual substance, for that consists of an idiom
which is still intelligible, still in common use. As is only fitting
in things of the mind, they see vanish one by one their every
chance of giving pleasure, and the very foundations of their
being collapse. Little by little those who loved them, who
appreciated them and were capable of understanding them,
disappear. Those who detested them, disparaged them and
mocked them are dead too. The passions which they aroused
are chilled. Other men thirst after or reject other books. Soon
what was meant to delight or to move becomes a Set Book in
schools. What was once true and beautiful becomes a dis-
ciplinary device or an object of enquiry — but of compulsory
enquiry. The unwilling enquirer, egged on by his sense of duty
and not by any pursuit of pleasure, peers at them in their
leathern or parchment tombs, only too aware that he is dis-
turbing them and bothering them, rather than reviving them,
that he is imparting to them, hopelessly and as it were reluc-
tantly, meanings and values as vain as they are artificial.
Sometimes Fashion, always and everywhere on the look-out for
copy for to-morrow's breakfast-table, finds a novelty in the
grave. For a brief moment it lifts the slab, dips in and then goes
its way. All that this sham interest achieves is to disfigure a
little further the sorry object of its restless enquiry. It makes
hardly any difference to the fact that something has vanished
for ever. All that Fashion can offer to the beauties of long ago,
in exchange for its sudden whim, is to be misunderstood.

Finally the very substance of what the mind has created —
a substance which is not corruptible in the ordinary sense of
the word, being unique in that it is made up of the most unsub-
stantial relationships imaginable — this substance of Language
is transformed without showing any outward change. It gets
out of touch with mankind. A word will become old-fashioned,
very rare, obscure in meaning, or will change its usage. Syntax
and idioms begin to show their age, surprise us and in the long
run put us off. *Tout s'achève en Sorbonne.*'

Everything ends as a subject for a D.Phil. thesis — or a Clark
Lecture.